StumbleUpon®

FOR

DUMMIES®

A Wiley Brand

JUL 13

by Steve Olenski and Nick Robinson

FOR

DUMMIES®

A Wiley Brand

StumbleUpon® For Dummies®

Published by:
John Wiley & Sons, Inc.,
111 River Street,
Hoboken, NJ 07030-5774,
www.wiley.com

Contents at a Glance

Table of Contents

Chapter 7: Sharing Your Discoveries and Content ...145

Chapter 8: Navigating the Recommended, Activity, Trending, and Lists Sections 155

Chapter 9: Using the Paid Discovery Advertising System 165

Chapter 10: Using StumbleUpon to Generate Traffic to Your Blog or Website 187

Introduction

*W*hether you've stumbled upon StumbleUpon previously or not, chances are you've at least heard of it — unless you've been living under a rock someplace.

Founded in 2001, StumbleUpon is a *discovery* engine, as opposed to those run-of-the-mill *search* engines out there like Google, Yahoo!, and so on. A discovery engine goes that extra mile by providing content to its users based on what said users want to see. Such a novel concept, right?

Users get to rate web pages, videos, photos, and every other kind of web-related content they come across. StumbleUpon then takes those individual ratings to generate related content back to the user. Say, for example, that you're just crazy about unicorns. (Nothing wrong with that, by the way — My Little Ponies, however, are a different matter.) Well, every time you give a favorable rating (or "thumbs up") to content about unicorns, the chances increase greatly that you'll see even more unicorn-related content as you Stumble.

With 25 million members and counting, StumbleUpon has become one of the most popular "websites" in the world. (We use quotes around that word because it is truly much more than just a website; it's really a combination website/platform/social media network/community.)

However it is described, on thing is clear: It is equally popular among brands and businesses as it is with the general public.

Many of StumbleUpon's users utilize the mobile apps, with recent statistics showing that out of the over 1 billion Stumbles per month, nearly 20 percent of them come from a mobile device.

And, of course, thanks to the mobile world we live in, the need to adapt accordingly was paramount, and StumbleUpon rose to the challenge, creating apps for both Android and iPhones alike.

About This Book

This book is for everyone in the entire free world! Okay, maybe not everyone. But it is for a whole lot of people — 25+ million StumbleUpon members and counting at last check.

This book introduces you to the wonder that is StumbleUpon — a site unlike any other where you can tailor your content to your specific Likes. So, if you happen to like, oh, let's say alligators, aardvarks, and avocadoes — the good folks at StumbleUpon will make sure that you see all the content on alligators, aardvarks, and avocadoes that you can!

Now, like anything else in life, one must crawl before he or she can run. And this book will help you ease your way (or your crawl) into StumbleUpon, and pretty soon you'll be up and running and fast becoming a Stumbler of epic proportions! Or something like that.

How This Book Is Organized

This book is organized into chapters covering such good stuff as using StumbleUpon on the Internet, on a mobile device, and in Windows 8. You also find out about StumbleUpon etiquette and the StumbleUpon bar.

If you're a StumbleUpon newbie, you can read this book from cover to cover as you begin Stumbling. Be sure to keep the book close by to serve as a reference or to guide you along your journey.

If you happen to be a StumbleUpon veteran, you can just go right to those chapters that can help keep you on your Stumbled toes, as it were. Hey, we all need a refresher course now and then, right?

Foolish Assumptions

You know what they say about assuming and assumptions, right?

Okay, we won't go there. But, having said that, we do have to make a few assumptions, as foolish as they may be.

One assumption we definitely make is that you know what a computer is, how to turn it on, how to use it, and how to use the Internet. We also assume that you know how to use social media networks such as Facebook, Twitter, and LinkedIn, in addition to using e-mail.

What we could not possibly assume or know is why you are reading this book. Only you know why you're reading it and why you want to use StumbleUpon. You may be using StumbleUpon for your personal pleasure. Great. Or you may be using it to help your business. Awesome. Or perhaps it's a little bit of both.

Whatever your individual reasons are, this book is here to help.

Icons Used in This Book

We use some basic icons throughout this book to help you quickly scan and find useful information and tips.

When you see the Tip icon, you're getting a quick tidbit of handy information on using StumbleUpon.

Some information is important to keep in mind as you use StumbleUpon, so when you see the Remember icon, be sure to tuck the information away for future reference.

Watch out! As with any online tool, you might need to avoid some pitfalls or do a vital task as you participate. Also, because StumbleUpon is always changing, we alert you to some potential issues in advance.

Where to Go from Here

We're all taught at a young age to start at the beginning, be it a story or a book or a movie.

This is no different. This book is best enjoyed from the beginning. But of course you're under no obligation to do so. On the contrary, feel free to dive into the deep end if you want. Just don't say we didn't warn you.

And, hey, if you ever need help along your Stumbling way, you can Like the Facebook page www.facebook.com/stumbleuponfor dummies or send a tweet to @steveolenski or @socialrobinson.

By all means, look us up on StumbleUpon, too, at www.stumble upon.com/stumbler/steveolenski or www.stumbleupon.com/stumbler/socialrobinson.

One last note: Please keep in mind that web interfaces can change at any moment and without notice. The overall concepts in this book apply no matter how StumbleUpon changes its interface. So know that we checked that all the information in this book was accurate as the book went to press, but some minor details in the steps and the way the website looks are likely to change. For major updates related to the book, you can also check out this book's web page at www.dummies.com/go/stumbleuponfdupdates.

Chapter 1

Getting Started on StumbleUpon

In This Chapter

▶ Say hello to StumbleUpon

▶ Registering your account

▶ Sharing what you stumble upon

*L*adies and gentlemen, get ready to start your engines . . . your StumbleUpon engines, that is.

StumbleUpon has become one of the most popular social media platforms around, and it doesn't hurt that it also happens to function as a search engine and bookmarking site. If you're looking to bring exposure to your content online — be it a website or blog post or whatever — StumbleUpon is where you want to be.

This chapter discusses how to register an account, set up your profile, share content, use StumbleUpon for business and marketing, and a whole lot more.

Introducing StumbleUpon

Unlike any other site or social media platform, StumbleUpon is unique in that it helps you, me, and anyone else who uses it find "stuff" — also known as "content." ("Content" is that fancy Internet word for "stuff.")

The best part is that the content that StumbleUpon brings essentially right to your front door is based on your personal Likes. The more content you give a "thumbs up" to — we cover exactly what a "thumbs up" means in future chapters — the more StumbleUpon knows about you and your Likes.

StumbleUpon then takes this information and uses it to come up with a pool of similar content so that when you Stumble, you're presented with content you're more likely to like.

Registering Your StumbleUpon Account

Registering your StumbleUpon account (creating it, in other words) is a very easy and fast process. It's so easy a caveman could . . . well, you get the idea.

Here are the steps to registering your StumbleUpon account:

1. **Visit** www.stumbleupon.com, **using your favorite web browser.**

2. **Click the big green Start Exploring button in the bottom middle of the screen. (See Figure 1-1.)**

   From here, you have the option to register your account with Facebook, and StumbleUpon will automatically create your username and password for you. Or, if you want to create your own username and password, you can go to the section marked "Or, Sign Up Using Email," where you can simply complete the brief form and then click the Sign Up button at the bottom of the screen. (See Figure 1-2.)

Figure 1-1: The Join for Free button.

If you were to click Connect With Facebook, you'd taken to a new screen (see Figure 1-3) where you could enter your Facebook login information to connect your StumbleUpon account to your Facebook account or, if you don't have a Facebook account, you could click the Sign up for Facebook link and that task would be taken care of for you.

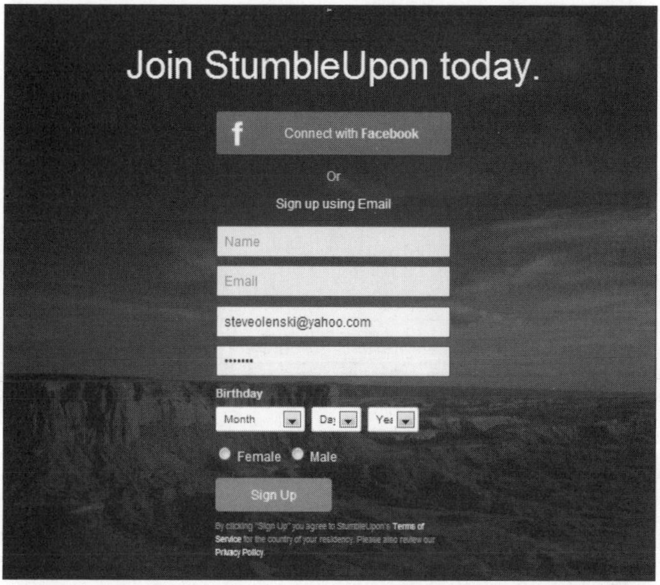

Figure 1-2: Use either Facebook or your e-mail to register a StumbleUpon account.

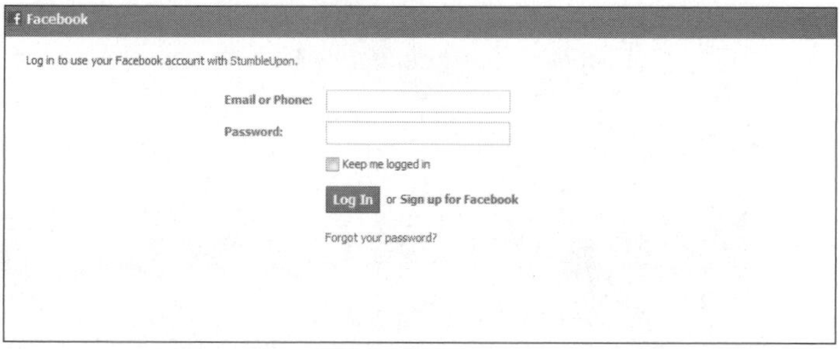

Figure 1-3: Signing up through Facebook.

3. **To complete your registration, just choose at least five of your favorite Interests from the list provided and then click the Save Interests button. (See Figure 1-4.)**

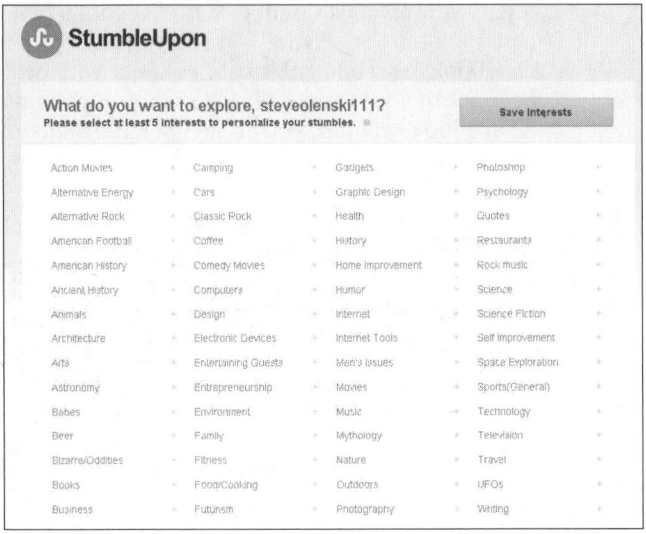

Figure 1-4: Your Initial Interests screen.

Setting Up Your Profile

If you've gone to the trouble of setting up your StumbleUpon account, the next thing you'll want to do is set up your profile. Here's how you'd do that:

1. **Sign in to your account and then check out your Home page.**

   While you're there, you'll see the word *Profile* along the top of the screen. (See Figure 1-5).

Look for Profile

Figure 1-5: The Profile link on your StumbleUpon home page.

2. Click Profile.

You'll be taken to your Profile page, where you'll see your registered StumbleUpon name alongside a silhouette image — that's where your Profile picture will eventually be. (See Figure 1-6).

Figure 1-6: How your Profile page appears right after creating your account.

3. Click the down arrow next to your account name in the upper-right corner.

Doing so brings up a series of options, including Settings. (See Figure 1-7).

Figure 1-7: A pull-down menu contains the Settings option.

4. Click Settings.

You are taken to the Settings page, which says Tell us a little about yourself along the top. (See Figure 1-8.)

5. Fill in the requested information and stuff about yourself, including your city and also a brief bio or description about yourself. Then click the Save Settings button.

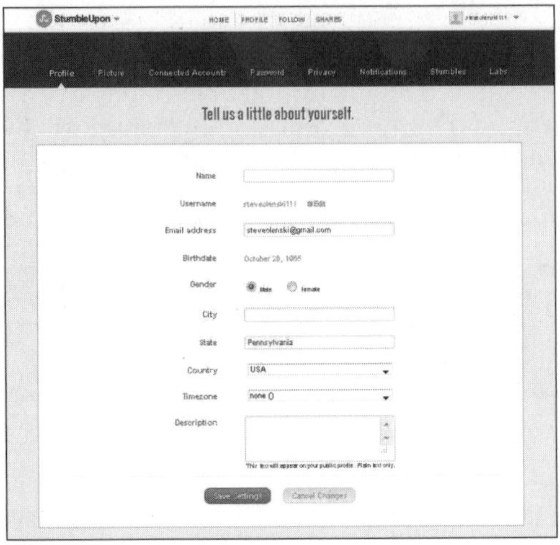

Figure 1-8: The Settings page.

Adding a Profile Picture

They say a picture is worth a thousand words, so when adding your profile picture, be sure to say a lot! Okay, we're kidding. To add a Profile picture, follow these steps:

1. **Head back to the Settings page and click the Picture link.**

   You find it along the top of the Settings page. (Refer to Figure 1-8.) For more on how to access the Settings page, check out the preceding section.

   After you click the Picture link, a Change Your Picture screen greets you, as shown in Figure 1-9.

2. **Using the Browse button, navigate to that corner of your hard drive that contains your fave photo of the moment and click to select it. Then click Next Step to upload your image.**

3. **(Optional) If desired, crop your profile picture to your specific preference. (See Figure 1-10.)**

4. **When you're happy with your image, click Save Picture.**

   You'll then be brought back to the Change Your Picture screen, only this time your saved picture will appear.

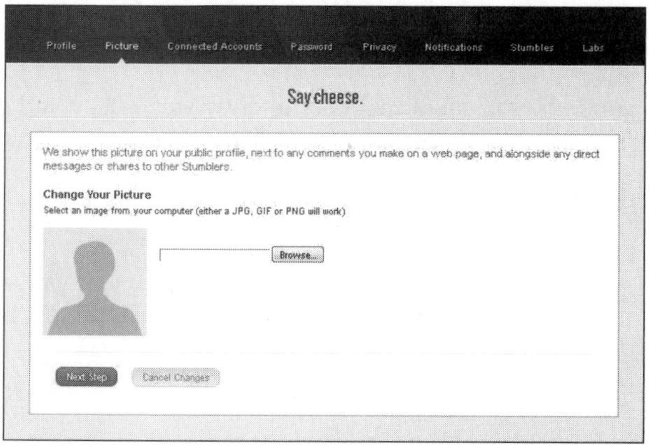

Figure 1-9: The Change Your Picture screen.

Figure 1-10: The Crop Your Picture screen.

Syncing StumbleUpon with Your Social Media Accounts

If you're like millions of other people out there, you probably already have a Facebook account, Twitter account, LinkedIn account, and/or Google account. And you'll more than likely want to sync your StumbleUpon account with all of them so that every-body's on the same page and sharing the same content.

The good news is, all of that can be done very easily and quickly! Here's how you sync StumbleUpon with your social media accounts:

1. **Click the Connected Accounts link found at the top of the Settings page. (See Figure 1-11.)**

   Doing so brings you to a screen where you can — what else? — connect your accounts. (See Figure 1-12.)

Click Connected Accounts

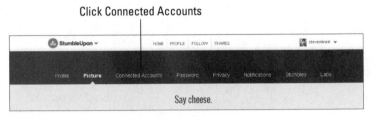

Figure 1-11: The Connected Accounts link.

Figure 1-12: Connecting your social media accounts.

2. **Click the Connect Your Account link that's associated with the desired social media network.**

   Clicking that link brings up a dialog box prompting you to allow StumbleUpon access to that account. (Figure 1-13 shows you what the prompt for the Facebook screen looks like.)

3. **Do whatever the prompt requires you to do to give StumbleUpon access to that account.**

   In the case of Facebook, a quick click of the Allow button means that your Facebook account and StumbleUpon account are synced — your activity on StumbleUpon shows up right on your Facebook timeline.

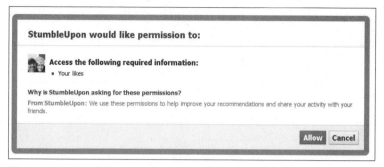

Figure 1-13: The Facebook permission screen.

Setting Your Notification Preferences

StumbleUpon has all sorts of cool ways to notify you of all kinds of different activities.

We're talking e-mail notifications, activity on StumbleUpon itself, and of course, mobile notifications. No matter how you want to be notified, StumbleUpon can do it. (Okay, maybe the carrier pigeon option is out, but pretty much everything else is possible.)

To set up your e-mail notification preferences so that StumbleUpon knows what's what, follow these steps:

1. **Click the Notifications link along the top of the screen on the Settings page. (See Figure 1-14.)**

    Doing so brings up a screen with the words "Stay up to date" along the top. (See Figure 1-15.)

The Notifications link

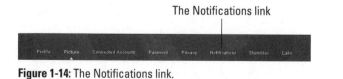

Figure 1-14: The Notifications link.

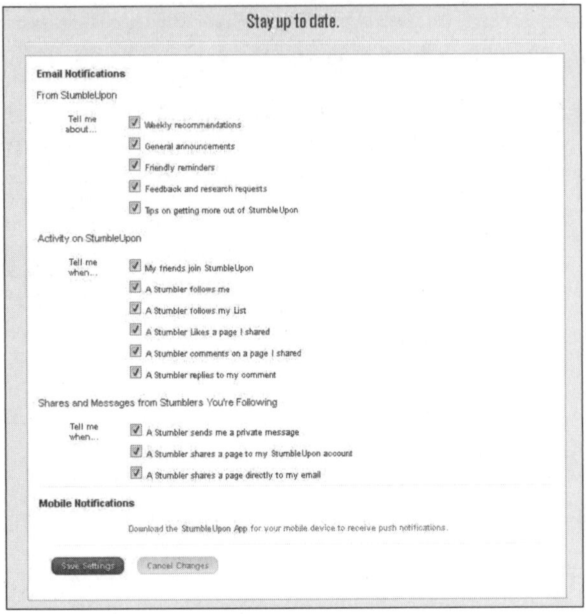

Figure 1-15: The Notifications Management screen.

2. **From this screen, you can control exactly when you want to be notified and what you want to be notified about.**

   For e-mail notifications, you can choose to be notified via three different options: From StumbleUpon, Activity on StumbleUpon, and Shares and Messages from Stumblers You're Following.

   • The From StumbleUpon section lets you specify the kinds of weekly e-mails you'll get from StumbleUpon, filled with recommendations on content that you may be interested in or tips on getting more out of StumbleUpon.

   • The Activity on StumbleUpon section has all your options when it comes to being informed about things happening in your account, including being notified when a friend on a social media network joins StumbleUpon or when a fellow Stumbler starts to follow you.

   • The Shares and Messages from Stumblers You're Following section lets you specify if and when you want to be notified via e-mail when a Stumbler sends you a private message or if a Stumbler shares a page directly to your e-mail.

Note the Mobile Notifications heading at the bottom of the screen, which you may have to scroll to see. Tucked away under this heading is the link that you'll want to use for downloading the StumbleUpon mobile app.

Refer to Chapters 4 and 5 for information that deals specifically with the StumbleUpon mobile app.

3. **When you're done setting your notification preferences, click the Save Settings button in the lower-left corner.**

Sharing Content

"Share and share alike" is an old saying. With StumbleUpon, you can not only share the awesome content you find on your Internet travels, but your StumbleUpon friends can also share what they find with you, too!

That is the easiest way to share content — by sharing it directly with your friends on StumbleUpon. To do this, you must be following each other, and if you are, there's no end to all the great stuff you can share.

To find out all about sharing content, including how to share your content across social media networks as well as with StumbleUpon friends, see Chapter 7.

Using StumbleUpon for Business and Marketing

If you own a business, chances are you also have a website. And if you have a website, chances are you want to drive as much traffic or views to your website as possible, all as a means to increase business.

Well, StumbleUpon is great when it comes to driving traffic, so it stands to reason that it's an incredibly valuable tool for any business owner or marketing professional.

The two most important words for today's business owners and marketers are *Content Marketing*. And StumbleUpon is truly a unique, easy, and cost-effective way to share your content with your customers and prospects alike.

See Chapters 9 and 10 for specific ways to use StumbleUpon to generate significantly more traffic to your website.

Chapter 2

Using StumbleUpon on the Internet

· ·

· ·

*F*uture chapters will discuss how to use StumbleUpon on mobile devices — smartphones, tablets, and so on. This chapter takes a different path by profiling how one could use StumbleUpon the "old-fashioned" way — by firing up the ol' web browser and cruising the Internet.

We say "old-fashioned" now, but it's getting to the point where using the Internet via a PC will soon become "ancient history," kind of like using typewriters and rotary phones. Seems like more and more of us are using our aforementioned smartphones and tablets to access our favorite sites, and (let's face it) apps are definitely cool.

But enough about that. This chapter is about Stumbling on the Internet. So get ready to rumb . . ., er, Stumble!

Adding and Following Interests

Before one can Stumble, he or she must first specify (or add) those particular StumbleUpon Interests that are, well, of interest to you.

Chapter 1 has a bit about how you specify your initial StumbleUpon Interests, so if you still need to do that, check out Chapter 1. (Figure 2-1 does a good job of showing the kinds of choices that are available to you.) If you've already specified some initial Interests and now want to add a few more to the mix, here's what you do:

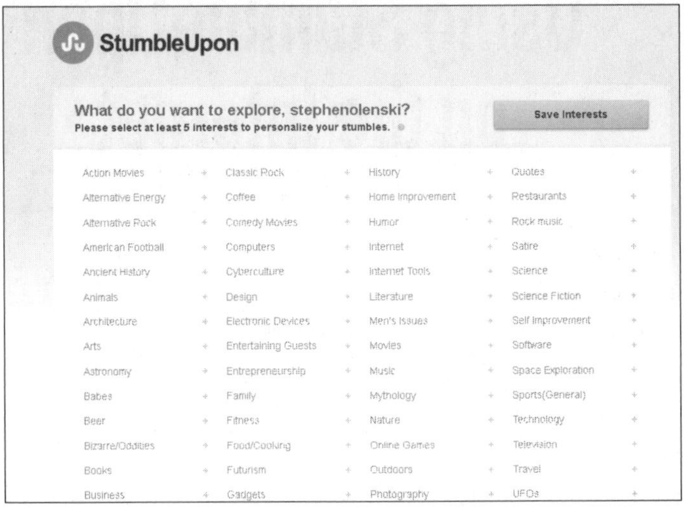

Figure 2-1: Your initial StumbleUpon Interests screen.

1. **From your StumbleUpon Home page, click the Add Interests button in the upper-right corner. (See Figure 2-2.)**

   Doing so brings up the Interests screen that you see in Figure 2-3. Note the three category headings near the center of the screen: All, Recommended, and Popular:

   • Clicking All brings up a list of all possible Interests you can add and follow.

   • Clicking Recommended brings up a list of sites selected by StumbleUpon specifically for you based on your current Interests.

   • Clicking Popular does what you expect — it brings up a list of the most popular Interests among all Stumblers.

The Add Interests button

Figure 2-2: The Add Interests button.

Your Interest options

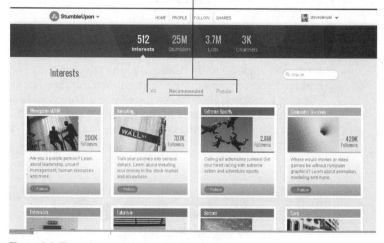

Figure 2-3: Three Interest options to choose from.

2. **Pick a category you like, and then click the Follow sign next to an Interest to add that Interest. That's all there is to it.**

Customizing your Interests via the Explore box

The folks at StumbleUpon came up with a great tool for those Stumblers who are dying to Stumble through additional content of particular interest to them — they call it the Explore box. It's great for Stumbling through hundreds of thousands of Interests without necessarily including these same Interests in your main Interest options.

To access the Explore box, go to the StumbleUpon home page if you are not currently there and just click the words `Explore an interest`, which are located directly above the Add Interests button. (Refer to Figure 2-2.)

In this box, all you need to do is type an interest, such as "puppies" or "baseball," and then hit Enter (or click the eyeglass icon).

Starting to Stumble

Okay, so you have your account all set up, your initial Interests options have been made, and you are ready to Stumble.

To do this, just go to the Home page at www.stumbleupon.com and click the orange-and-white Stumble icon. (See Figure 2-4.) Clicking this icon takes you to a website that may at first seem random but is, in fact, one personally plucked out of that immense haystack that is the Internet for you by StumbleUpon based on your Interests.

The StumbleUpon icon

Figure 2-4: The StumbleUpon icon.

You have the following additional ways to Stumble:

✔ **Via the StumbleBar:** Refer to Chapter 3 for instructions on using the StumbleBar.

✔ **By Stumbling your Likes:** Likes are a bit different than Interests insomuch as these are the pages that you have given a "thumbs up" to in the past.

To Stumble your Likes, you must first access your profile. To do so, do the following:

a. *Click the small down arrow next to your name on your Home page.* (You can see it there in Figure 2-5 right above the Explore an Interest field.)

Doing so opens a drop-down menu with a number of options, including a View Profile option. (See Figure 2-6.)

b. *Click to select the View Profiles option.*

A new screen appears. Note the orange-and-white box with the words Stumble Your Likes in it. (See Figure 2-7.)

c. *Click Stumble Your Likes.*

Doing so brings up content based on those pages you previously liked.

The down arrow

Figure 2-5: Look for the small down arrow next to your name.

Figure 2-6: The View Profile option.

The Stumble Your Likes button

Figure 2-7: The Stumble Your Likes button.

For more information on how to work with Likes and Dislikes, check out Chapter 3.

Submitting content to StumbleUpon for others to share

So, perhaps you have your own website (or a specific page on your website) that you'd just love to submit to StumbleUpon for your fellow Stumblers to see and hopefully share and give a thumbs up to.

Here's how you submit that content:

1. **Back on your Home page, click the down arrow next to your name. (Refer to Figure 2-5.)**

2. **From the options that appear, click Add a Page. (Refer to Figure 2-6.)**

The Add a New Page screen appears, as shown in
Figure 2-8.

3. **Using the Add a New Page screen, enter the** *URL* **(the web
page address, in other words) of the page you want to
submit along with the following additional information:**

Figure 2-8: The Add a New Page screen.

- *Is this page safe for work?* Remember that some of your
  fellow Stumblers may open this site on a work-issued
  computer, and you don't want them getting into trouble
  looking at a site that is not suitable or even allowed on
  their work PC.

- *What's this page about?* Clicking the Select an Interest
  down arrow brings up a list of topics to choose from.

- *Add Tags (optional).* In this box, you can enter specific tags or keywords that you want to include. These
  can help Stumblers find your content based on those
  same tags and keywords. You can also enter additional
  Interests in this box because you can only choose one in
  the previous section. For example, if your site deals with
  marketing and advertising, you can choose Marketing
  from the Select an Interest box then add Advertising to
  the Add Tags box.

- *Write a comment (optional).* In this section, you can add
  a description about the particular content you're sharing. This will help the reader have a better understand-
  ing of the content in addition to only seeing the title.

- *What's the page's language?* Pretty self-explanatory. Just
  choose the language that this particular content is written in.

4. **After inputting all the above information, the last step is to click the Add This Page button and StumbleUpon will take it from there.**

Finding follow-worthy folks on StumbleUpon

Hey, this is social media, after all and, as such, you want to find other StumbleUpon users to connect with, right? Of course you do!

Here's how to do that:

1. **Click Follow in the top center of your Home page. (See Figure 2-9.)**

   A new screen appears with options along the top including Stumblers. (See Figure 2-10.)

Click Follow

Figure 2-9: Look for the Follow option.

Figure 2-10: Options to click, including Stumblers.

2. **Click Stumblers.**

   When you click Stumblers for the first time, a screen greets you in which the nice folks at StumbleUpon ask for more information about you. (See Figure 2-11.) This information helps them help you find folks with similar interests on StumbleUpon.

3. What you need now is to go forth and Stumble content that you like, rating content with a thumbs up or thumbs down along the way

4. When you come back in, say, two weeks' time and then click Stumblers again, you'll see a list of Stumblers that StumbleUpon recommends just for you.

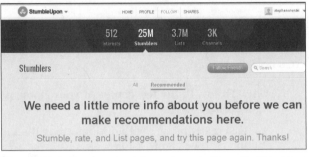

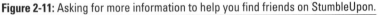

Figure 2-11: Asking for more information to help you find friends on StumbleUpon.

Finding folks you already know on social media networks

To find those social media friends and family on Facebook, LinkedIn, Twitter, and Google who also use StumbleUpon, you must first connect your various social media accounts to your StumbleUpon account.

Refer to Chapter 7 for information on how to connect your social media accounts to your StumbleUpon accounts.

After you have your social media and StumbleUpon accounts connected, go back to your Home page and click Follow at the top center (refer to Figure 2-9). When you click Stumblers at the top of the new screen that appears (refer to Figure 2-10), you'll now see all those Facebook friends of yours who are also on StumbleUpon.

Finding folks you already know via their e-mail account(s)

Another quick way to track down those friends and family members who are also Stumblers is by locating them via their e-mail account(s).

The reason we use the word *account(s)* with the *s* at the end is that many people today have more than one e-mail account. And you may not know which one they used to set up their StumbleUpon account.

To search and find your friends via e-mail on StumbleUpon, just type in their e-mail address in the search field on the Follow screen, which is located directly to the right of the Follow Friends button, and then press Enter. (See Figure 2-12.)

The e-mail search field

Figure 2-12: The search field located right next to Follow Friends.

Inviting friends to StumbleUpon

You know just how great StumbleUpon really is, so naturally you want to tell all your friends how great it is, too, and invite them to join you! Piece of cake.

In the section "Finding folks you already know on social media networks," earlier in this chapter, we told you how to find your fellow social media friends who are also on StumbleUpon.

However, as hard as it may be to believe, some of your friends might not be on StumbleUpon. Shocking, right? Well here's how to fix that.

After you connect your various social media accounts and click Stumblers, in addition to seeing your friends who *are* on StumbleUpon, Facebook, and so on, you'll also see a group of friends who are not.

After you click to select which of your Facebook friends you want to invite to StumbleUpon, click Continue (see Figure 2-13) and a new pop-up window appears. (See Figure 2-14.)

Figure 2-13: Invite your Facebook friends to StumbleUpon.

Figure 2-14: A Facebook pop-up window with a StumbleUpon request.

In this window, you will see the list of people you are inviting, along with a prewritten message asking them to join you on StumbleUpon. The only thing left to do is to click the Send Requests button.

With Facebook out of the way, you can move on to Twitter. Just click Continue. Then from the next screen, click the Twitter icon. (See Figure 2-15.) The screen you come to next is the Twitter Authorization screen. (See Figure 2-16.) On this screen, you must click the Authorize App button before proceeding. Doing so brings up a new screen that shows all your Twitter followers who are already on StumbleUpon and a section with a prewritten message that you can then tweet to your followers, inviting them to follow you on StumbleUpon. (See Figure 2-17.)

Click Continue and — just like that — a Tweet is sent out to all your followers.

Figure 2-15: The Twitter option.

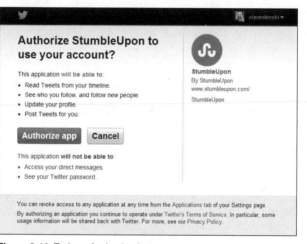

Figure 2-16: Twitter Authorization screen.

Figure 2-17: A prewritten tweet inviting your Twitter followers to follow you on StumbleUpon.

You can alter the tweet to your liking, but just remember the 140-character limit on Twitter. After tweeting out the message to your Twitter followers, you then come to another screen. (See Figure 2-18.)

Figure 2-18: Screen that appears after inviting people to follow you on StumbleUpon via Twitter.

From this screen, you can choose to invite your fellow Google friends to follow you on StumbleUpon (or invite more via Facebook).

Similar to Facebook, when you click the Google icon, you're brought to a list of people you are connected to via Google so that you can invite them to join StumbleUpon.

After selecting those folks you want to invite from Google, click Continue and you're brought to yet another new screen with a message stating that you've invited this person(s) to join you on StumbleUpon. (See Figure 2-19.)

This same screen, however, has an option for inviting people via regular, old e-mail — not the hopped-up Google version, in other words. Click the Other Email icon and you are brought to a new screen. (See Figure 2-20.)

From here you can use the form to invite up to three people at a time via e-mail to follow you on StumbleUpon.

You will see a prewritten message just as in the Facebook, Twitter, and Google options. Like Twitter, you have the option to alter the e-mail message before clicking that Send Now button.

Figure 2-19: Screen that appears after inviting people via Google.

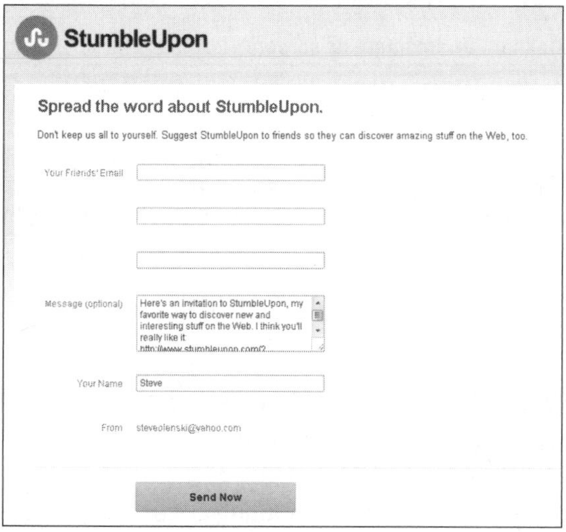

Figure 2-20: The Invite via Email screen.

Removing Interests

Hey, life changes and so, too, can your Interests. So at some time, you may want to stop seeing Stumbles from an interest you previously were just mad about. This is completely your option and doing so is very easy.

The first thing to do is go to your Profile page, so go ahead and click that down arrow next your name in the upper-right corner of your Home page and choose View Profile from the menu that appears. (Refer to Figure 2-6.)

After you are on your Profile page, click Interests. (Refer to Figure 2-7; you see Interests right above the Add a Page button.) Up will come all your current Interests, as shown in Figure 2-21.

Figure 2-21: Your current Interests screen.

To remove an interest so that it no longer appears in your StumbleUpon stream in the future, simply mouse over the word "Following" next to that particular interest. The word "Unfollow" will appear along with an "X." Just click the X and that Interest will no longer be followed.

That's all there is to it. Told you it was easy.

Encountering "No more Interests in a given Interest"

At some point, during your Stumbling adventures, you may come upon a message stating that you have "run out of Stumbles" or "you have Stumbled all pages in this Interest."

Now, this is not a sign that the world is ending, so please don't worry about that. Read on to find out what it *really* means.

What it means

Well, like we said, the world is not coming to an end. It just means that StumbleUpon does not have enough information on you (yet) to keep providing you with the content you want to see.

The more you like and dislike a Stumble, the better StumbleUpon can get to know you and your Interests.

The more you tell StumbleUpon, the better it can determine just the right content for you as you Stumble along your merry way.

What to do next

The best thing to do is to keep liking and disliking content. StumbleUpon recommends that you like or dislike a minimum of 10 percent of all your Stumbles to get the best results.

Another thing you can do is simply add more Interests. With so many to choose from, there's bound to be some that you may not even be aware of because of the amount of Interests in general or the fact that new Interests are added all the time.

One final thing to do is find and follow your fellow Stumblers who share an interest in the same Interests that you do.

All these strategies help ensure that your StumbleUpon content well never runs dry.

Deleting your account

A day may come when you decide that you and StumbleUpon must each go your separate ways. (Perhaps you've decided to join that Buddhist monastery on Mount Baldy.) To delete your StumbleUpon account, you need to be signed in to your account.

From there, follow these steps:

1. **Click the down arrow next to your name on your Home page. (Refer to Figure 2-5.)**

2. **Choose Settings from the menu of options that appears. (Refer to Figure 2-6.)**

3. **On the screen that appears, click Privacy. (See Figure 2-22.)**

Click Privacy

Figure 2-22: Options along the top of the screen include Privacy.

4. Next to the words *Delete Account* **(see Figure 2-23), click the orange Click Here to Initiate Account Deletion link.**

Doing so takes you to another screen where you're asked to provide your password before submitting your request for the account to be deleted. (See Figure 2-24.)

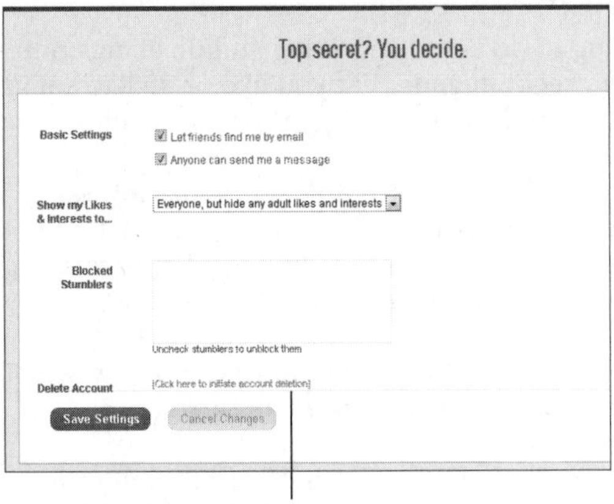

Click here to initiate account deletion

Figure 2-23: Screen showing the Delete Account option.

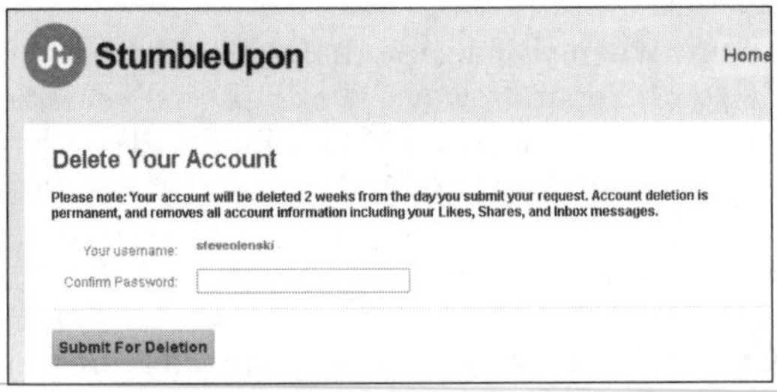

Figure 2-24: The Delete Your Account screen.

5. Enter your password and then click Submit for Deletion.

The process to delete your StumbleUpon account begins. You'll be notified via e-mail when the process is complete.

Important things to know when deleting your account

While we surely don't want to see you go, remember the following key items when deleting your StumbleUpon account:

✔ The only person who can delete a StumbleUpon account is the person who is linked to the e-mail account used to open that account. The folks at StumbleUpon are not permitted to delete an account.

✔ Deleting an account means that all your personal information as well as your profile will be permanently removed.

✔ Your StumbleUpon account will be deleted 14 days after your initial deletion request.

✔ During this 14-day time frame, however, you are allowed to reactivate your account.

✔ When you delete your account, you will no longer be able to use your previous username on a new account should you want to set up a new account in the future.

✔ If you want to just change your e-mail address on the account or even your username, you do not need to delete your account. You can do all this via the Settings section in your profile.

✔ To use the e-mail address from an account you are deleting on another StumbleUpon account, first be sure to change the e-mail on the account you are deleting to something else so you can use that e-mail for another account.

Creating more than one StumbleUpon account

Per the StumbleUpon Terms of Service, you are not permitted to have more than one account per member/profile. And each StumbleUpon account should only be used by the owner of that account.

However, if you want to create more than one entirely separate StumbleUpon account, you are allowed to do that. Should you decide to create more than one account, be sure that each account is signed out before logging in to the other account.

A work-around for this is to log in to each separate account on different browsers: Firefox, Chrome, Internet Explorer, and so on.

Merging two accounts

At present, you cannot combine more than two StumbleUpon accounts. Here's the best thing to do: If you end up with more than one account, keep the account that has more Likes and Interests on it. It just makes more sense to keep the account that has more activity on it.

Participating in StumbleUpon labs

The folks at StumbleUpon are always trying out new ideas, new ways and methods to make the Stumbling experience the best it can possibly be.

The way they do that is by working directly with Stumblers just like you who can go out and "test-drive" some not-released-to-the-general-public features and provide feedback on them.

To participate in StumbleUpon labs, just click Labs on your Settings page. You'll see some new features that are in development or "beta" phase. Select the check box next to each feature that you want to try. Then click Save Settings and start Stumbling.

At times, no new features are available via the StumbleUpon labs. If that is the case when you visit the Labs page, be sure to check back from time to time to see whether any have been added.

Chapter 3

Using the StumbleBar Toolbar

*N*ow that you are living in 2013, you're probably used to smartphones, high-speed Internet connections, and of course, access to the biggest library of content in the history of the world! Having access to all this information comes at a price though: your time.

It takes some time to switch from one site to another when looking for and sharing information. Why not bring the StumbleUpon experience to every site that you visit? It is possible, and over the course of this book, we definitely show you how.

A big part of "showing you how" involves getting you acquainted with the StumbleBar, a great asset in your quest to become a true StumbleUpon machine.

Installing the StumbleBar

Chapters 1 and 2 make you aware (in general terms) of this great timesaving tool that StumbleUpon provides. Now it's time to get down to some nuts-and-bolts stuff — which right now means getting the StumbleBar installed on your Internet browser.

Don't worry, we know that you're probably partial to a particular Internet browser, which is precisely why we're going to show you how to install the StumbleBar on Chrome and Firefox. We have you covered!

REMEMBER

Unfortunately for you Mac Safari users, StumbleUpon does not currently support the StumbleBar for Safari.

Point your Internet browser of choice to www.stumbleupon.com/downloads. You'll be greeted by the page you see in Figure 3-1, which gives you several options for downloading the StumbleBar, each tailored to a specific browser. See, we told you we had you covered!

Figure 3-1: Here you see the main download page for the StumbleBar.

Bookmarking the StumbleUpon button

First things first. We know that you're going to want to Stumble first thing in the morning, so to save time, you'll want to drag a special link to Stumble onto your browser's Bookmarks toolbar. (The Internet term for such a special link is *bookmark,* so what you are doing is *bookmarking* Stumble for later use.) On the StumbleUpon Downloads page (refer to Figure 3-1), you'll notice that the first download item in the list is a bookmark link to StumbleUpon. Just drag that hyperlink — named, appropriately enough "StumbleUpon" — to the Bookmarks toolbar of your Internet browser. In Figure 3-2, you see what the button looks like when placed in Firefox.

In IE10 on Windows 8, the Bookmarks toolbar is called "Favorites" and is hidden by default. You'll need to enable the Favorites toolbar.

A bookmarked Stumble button

Figure 3-2: The StumbleUpon button appears at the top of your browser near the bookmark section in Firefox.

After you successfully place the StumbleUpon button on your browser Bookmarks toolbar, all you have to do is click the button and you automatically Stumble. You will thank me for this later.

Installing the StumbleBar for Chrome

Okay, you have that shiny new StumbleUpon button on your browser Bookmarks toolbar. Now it's time for the real work of this chapter — installing the StumbleBar. If your browser of choice is the Chrome browser and you want to do all your Stumbling by using the StumbleBar for Chrome, go yet again to `www.stumble upon.com/downloads` and click the Download the Extension link underneath the StumbleBar for Chrome (PC and Mac) heading.

The next page is an overview of what you're actually downloading into Chrome. Here you find details about the Chrome extension, as well as reviews by other users. After you browse around, click the Add to Chrome button in the upper-right corner, as shown in Figure 3-3.

On the next screen, a window pops up asking (quite politely) "Add StumbleUpon?" The extension asks nicely because it needs your permission to access your data on all websites (including all tab/browsing activity) to function as planned. Go ahead and click Add.

After the StumbleBar is downloaded, a new tab with the StumbleUpon Sign In page opens. Sign in to StumbleUpon, using the username/e-mail and password you created when first signing up for the account.

After you are signed in to your account, you have successfully downloaded the StumbleBar for Chrome. Figure 3-4 shows you what the StumbleBar looks like after successfully downloading the extension.

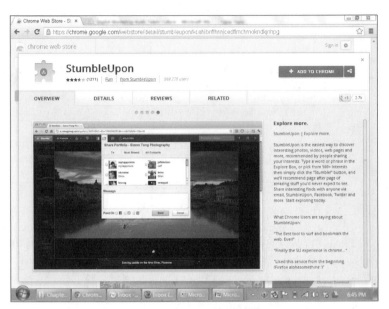

Figure 3-3: Click the Add to Chrome button to begin the StumbleBar installation process.

The StumbleBar for Chrome

Figure 3-4: You can see what the StumbleBar looks like after going through the Chrome installation process.

Installing the StumbleBar for Firefox

To see how things would work if you're partial to the Firefox browser and would prefer a Firefox-specific StumbleBar, go to (you guessed it) www.stumbleupon.com/downloads and click the Download the Add-on link underneath the StumbleBar for Firefox (PC and Mac) heading. (Refer to Figure 3-1.)

The next page (see Figure 3-5) is an overview of what you are downloading into Firefox. Feel free to browse the reviews to get others' take on the Firefox version of StumbleBar. After convincing yourself of the extension's value, go ahead and click the Add to Firefox button.

Figure 3-5: Click the Add to Firefox button to get started with the StumbleBar installation process.

On the next screen, a warning dialog box pops up with the message Install add-ons only from authors whom you trust. Don't worry, it's in StumbleUpon's best interests not to infect your devices with malicious software. Go ahead and click Install Now.

After the StumbleBar is downloaded, you see a dialog box pop up that says StumbleUpon will be installed after you restart Firefox. Go ahead and click Restart Now.

After Firefox restarts, you see new features at the top of your browser, as shown in Figure 3-6. Make sure to sign in to start using the StumbleBar by clicking the Sign-In button there at the top and typing in your login details.

The StumbleBar for Firefox

Figure 3-6: Sign in to StumbleUpon to start using the StumbleBar in Firefox.

Putting That New StumbleBar to Use

Now that your StumbleBar is installed, it's time to take advantage of what it can offer. Before you explore, though, it's important that you understand the basic functions of the StumbleBar and what they mean for you and the StumbleUpon community.

Liking and disliking content

OK, here's my StumbleUpon regimen. We are big proponents of reading a long line of articles first thing in the morning. Personally, it provides a spark and gets our creative juices flowing.

When sitting at our computers first thing in the morning, we fire up our Firefox browsers and sign in to StumbleUpon with the help of our trusty StumbleBar. Next, we click Stumble, and we're taken to a web page that StumbleUpon deems worthy of our viewing — potentially uncharted territory, but StumbleUpon usually knows what it is doing.

After reading an article that we really like, naturally we want to show our approval by clicking I Like It! on the StumbleBar toolbar. The benefit to you for liking content is that you teach StumbleUpon to serve more content like what you just "liked." Over time, StumbleUpon is better able to gauge what could potentially float your boat, so your experience within StumbleUpon will become more and more personalized.

Conversely, if you read a piece of content that you really don't like, you can click the Thumbs Down icon on the toolbar. If you hover your mouse over the icon, it will say `No more like this`. Essentially, you continue to teach StumbleUpon about your personal preferences. You are essentially saying, "Hey, StumbleUpon, stop serving me this type of stuff!"

With that little exposé of the benefits of liking and disliking content out of the way, we now take you through an example by using a real-world article.

We just clicked the Stumble button on our StumbleBar and are now reading an article called "Jedi Mind Tricks: 17 Lesser Known Ways to Persuade People." We're big fans of consumer behavior, so we give it a like. After clicking I Like It!, the Thumbs Up icon turns green, as shown in Figure 3-7. (Well, you could see the green if this book had color illustrations; Guess you'll just have to trust us on this one.)

Maybe you're not a big fan of consumer behavior, and you really don't want to see more content like this. Simply click the Thumbs Down icon and it turns red (or blue in Chrome). That's all there is to it!

In Firefox, if you accidentally click the Thumbs Down icon, don't worry. You can undo this by clicking the drop-down arrow next to the icon. Simply click the check mark, and the red Thumbs Down icon turns blue. (In Chrome, you see a submenu with a whole bunch of options when you click on the Thumbs Down icon.)

The I Like It! button

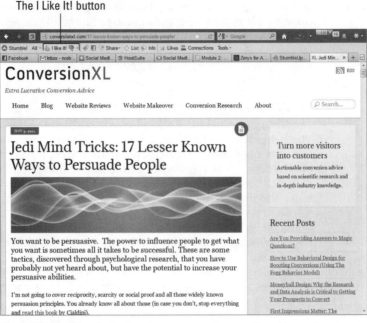

Figure 3-7: The Thumbs Up icon turns green when you like a piece of content, using the StumbleBar.

Commenting on content

Picture this. You're reading an article and it really strikes a chord with you. You're so passionate about the subject, in fact, that you can't help but leave a comment with words of encouragement.

The StumbleBar makes this easy with one click of a mouse, some keyboard strokes, and a final confirmation.

Again, when you leave comments, StumbleUpon continues to learn what types of content to serve. Whether your comments are negative or positive, StumbleUpon will give more weight to pieces of content with comments than it will with likes.

Think about it from StumbleUpon's point of view. It takes more effort to leave a comment than it does to click a Like or Dislike button, so the content is more likely to resonate with more members of the StumbleUpon community.

Need an example? Here's one. (To keep things simple, we're using the same article as the previous example, "Jedi Mind Tricks: 17 Lesser Known Ways to Persuade People.")

Click the Info bubble icon on the StumbleBar toolbar, and you are taken to a page that shows all the people who have liked the content as well as their comments. Click the bubble icon next to the content graphic at the top of the page, as shown in Figure 3-8.

In Chrome, after you click on the bubble icon, you see a comment pop-up you can use to leave a comment.

Still in Firefox, you'll see a window pop up with the comments of other folks embedded. At the bottom of that window, click in the text box and type your comment, as shown in Figure 3-9. After you're finished typing your comment, click Post. Now your comment is submitted for the world to see. Wasn't that easy?

Click here to leave a comment.

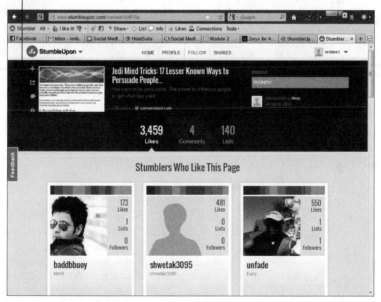

Figure 3-8: Click the bubble icon next to the content graphic at the top of the page to leave a comment.

Don't leave comments that you wouldn't want showing up next to your own content. Play by the rules, and you will gain the trust of the StumbleUpon community.

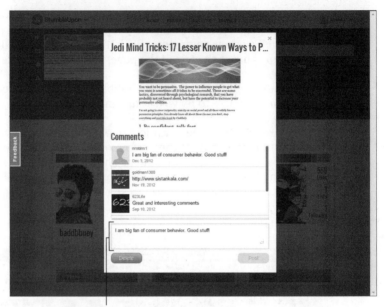

Add your comment here.

Figure 3-9: Click in the text box and type your comment. Then click Post to submit your comment.

Expanding your reach with social media

You know it as well as we do. You have less time nowadays, so anything that helps you be more efficient is a blessing.

In addition to creating efficiency, the StumbleBar creates a fluid social experience while you view content. What this means is that you can actively participate in the StumbleUpon community without having to go through the extra step of opening a different browser window or tab.

The StumbleBar even goes beyond StumbleUpon and allows you to share content with friends in other social networks, while remaining inside StumbleUpon proper. In a sense, you get to make all the other social networks part of your StumbleUpon experience.

For example, you can share with friends via

✔ Facebook

✔ Twitter

✔ E-mail

Being able to rely on these other "delivery systems" makes it so much easier for you to spread outstanding content to people who aren't necessarily StumbleUpon savvy. Rather than copying and pasting a web address into e-mails, and then Facebook, and then Twitter, you complete the steps in one quick motion.

Keeping your content organized

If you're the type of person who likes to organize a vault of content for later use, the StumbleBar is your perfect companion. For any piece of content that you Stumble across, the StumbleBar allows you to add tags and create lists seamlessly without having to go to Stumbleupon.com.

Tags are keywords that you add to a web page to better organize all the pages that you've interacted with in StumbleUpon. For example, we add tags such as "blogging" and "content development" to content that teaches us how to produce content more efficiently. (You find out how to add tags in the next section.)

Lists are used in StumbleUpon to organize your content into categories. For example, we could create a list called "Marketing Automation" to hold all articles that explain the subject. Take another example: Say that you have a big project coming up about the history of your city. You can then set up a list entitled "History Project" and add different types of content to that list. (You're allowed to be creative with the titles of your lists, so let your imagination run wild.) (Again, you find out how to set up lists in the next section.)

All in all, you aren't taking advantage of the many benefits that StumbleUpon provides if you don't use the StumbleBar. So why not give it a try? We promise you that your social networking life will be more efficient, organized, and fluid as you traverse the interwebs.

Understanding the StumbleBar icons

At first glance, the StumbleBar can make you dizzy with all the icons to keep track of. Never fear! In this section, we walk you through what each icon stands for and what it does. Use this section as a reference in case you're ever confused by the variety of icons at any point after downloading the StumbleBar.

By default, the main Stumble button is on the far left of the StumbleBar toolbar; this is where you start exploring websites within the categories you specify when setting up your profile.

To drill down into more specific content, like photos or videos, click the drop-down arrow labeled All, right next to the main StumbleBar button. As shown in Figure 3-10, you have a ton of options to choose from. For example, if you only want to Stumble pictures, select Photos from the drop-down menu that appears. Immediately after you click, StumbleUpon takes you to a Photo page. Every time you click Stumble thereafter, you're taken to a web page with a prominent photo.

If you're using Chrome, you aren't provided with the customization that Firefox offers. If you find that certain icons described in this section don't exist in Chrome, they are available in Firefox.

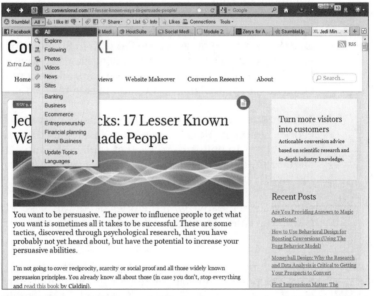

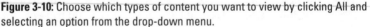

Figure 3-10: Choose which types of content you want to view by clicking All and selecting an option from the drop-down menu.

To revert to the default Stumble setting, click the button next to the main Stumble button — it may be labeled Photos or News or Video or whatever else you selected last — and select All from the drop-down menu that appears.

You have other options on the drop-down menu in addition to different content types, as the following list makes clear:

- ✔ Interest categories specified during the initial profile setup.
- ✔ Stumble pages in foreign languages.

✔ Sites from people you are following. (See Chapter 2 for an explanation of "following.")

✔ An Explore option that lets you manually search the web by taking you straight to a search page.

✔ Update Interests by clicking the button where you will be taken to a page to update your preferred Interests. These are the Interests you chose when registering with StumbleUpon.

Continuing your tour of the StumbleBar icons, the next two — going from left to right — are the by-now familiar Like and Dislike icons. If you enjoy the content you're viewing, click the Like icon — the Thumbs Up icon. If you're not a big fan of the content you are viewing, feel free to click the Dislike icon — the one with the thumbs down.

If you're a sharing type, the next two icons will stick out. Click the Facebook symbol to share the web page with your Facebook friends. Quite simple.

If you guessed that the Tag icon had something to do with organizing content by "tags" or keywords, as spelled out in the preceding section, you hit the nail on the head. Keeping your content organized with the help of the Tag icon is especially helpful if you like to refer back to old pieces of content. For example, if you regularly consume different types of art content, you can use different tags to distinguish between types of art. For Picasso content, you use the tag "Picasso," and for Rembrandt content, you use the tag "Rembrandt." Starting to make sense?

Let's say that you want to find the Rembrandt content two weeks from now. First, click on "Profile" on the homepage of StumbleUpon when signed in. Next, in the Search box, type Rembrandt, and all the Rembrandt content you tagged previously will show up. Easy as pie!

Chrome doesn't include the tag icon.

The button with the envelope and a green arrow is the more comprehensive Share button. When you click Share, a drop-down menu gives you several options, as shown in Figure 3-11.

Facebook is so nice, it gets listed twice — as its own icon and as part of the drop-down. If you're a Twitter lover, the Twitter icon allows you to tweet the piece of content with a special StumbleUpon-shortened link.

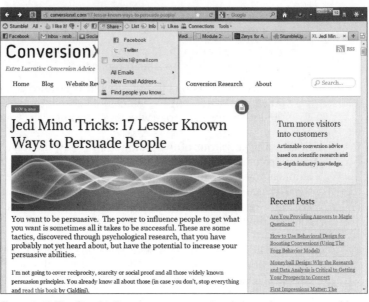

Figure 3-11: The StumbleBar gives you several options to share content with other social networks within the StumbleUpon experience.

Sometimes, you feel more comfortable sending a piece of content to someone by e-mail. All you do is click All Emails on the drop-down menu and then click inside the box to the left of an e-mail address that you added to the StumbleBar. Doing so brings up a Send button. Click Send and a box will appear where you can enter a customized subject. Then simply click Send again.

If you haven't added any e-mails to your StumbleBar, click New Email Address on the drop-down menu and type in the e-mail address of the person with whom you want to share the piece of content. (After entering any new e-mail address, that address appears in the drop-down menu's All Emails listing.)

If you want to add more people to your e-mail list within StumbleUpon, select the Find People You Know item from the Share drop-down menu. You have the option of finding people you are connected to on Facebook, Twitter, and Google. Simply click one of the three options and follow the instructions that each network provides.

Continuing my little tour, the next icon — the plus sign — stands for lists. Lists are used in StumbleUpon to organize your content into distinct categories. For example, we could create a list called

"HTML Tutorials" for all articles that explain the subject. For another example, say that you have a big project coming up about new forms of social media marketing. You add different types of content into a list called "Marketing Project." You're allowed to be creative with the title of your lists.

If you're the organizing type, click List and a dialog box will pop up. Simply enter the name of the list if you have already created one. If you don't have any lists yet, this is the perfect time to create a new one. When you finish typing the name of the list, click the Create New link under the text field, as shown in Figure 3-12. To add new content to a list, go to a web page related to your list — say, a page about HTML Coding. Go to the page, click the + icon, and then choose the appropriate list from the menu that appears. Voila, you're done!

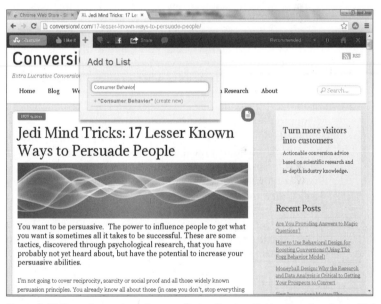

Figure 3-12: Organize content that you find online by clicking the plus sign, which stands for Lists.

The Info icon — the one sporting a speech bubble — is useful if you want to view more social activity around a piece of content. When you click the Info icon, you come to a page where you can view all users who have liked, commented upon, or added the article to a list.

The Likes icon — the one sporting a star — shows you all content that you have liked on a single page. From there, StumbleUpon gives you flexibility to refine your search by using several criteria, including the following:

- ✔ Photos
- ✔ Videos
- ✔ Additions
- ✔ By Interest

If you have "tagged" your content, type commonly used tags in the Search box within your profile page to find what you're looking for.

The Connections icon — look for the one with two people, one person wearing a blue shirt and the other wearing a red shirt — lets you view all the people you're following. Think of "following" someone on StumbleUpon as you would "follow" someone's activity in a social network. You can see all the content he likes, comment on that content, and send him private messages. The Connections icon is helpful when connecting with people to whom you haven't spoken in a while.

The next icon is for notifications and messages — either from the folks at StumbleUpon or from others in your StumbleUpon community. In Chrome, this will show up as a number and in Firefox and IE, it will show up as a tiny mailbox, as shown in Figure 3-13. When you are a very active member of the StumbleUpon community, you will check this often.

Many other customizations exist for your StumbleBar, but we suggest sticking with the basic options as you get accustomed to the different icon functions.

Now that the installation of the StumbleBar is complete, it is time to explore the web and interact in the community. Go out there and have some fun!

Notifications and messages

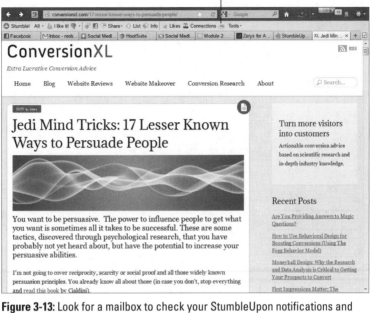

Figure 3-13: Look for a mailbox to check your StumbleUpon notifications and messages.

Chapter 4

Using StumbleUpon on Your iPhone or iPad

*L*ike many other social media platforms, StumbleUpon is available for use on mobile devices such as the iPhone and iPad. The StumbleUpon iPhone app and iPad app received critical acclaim within the industry, scoring 4 and 4.5 stars out of 5, respectively, from the editors at *PC Magazine*.

They referred to the StumbleUpon iPhone app as a "great way to explore the Web" and labeled the iPad app as "one of the best apps for the iPad, period." And just like the web-based version, the iPhone and iPad StumbleUpon apps allow you to share fascinating and interesting content from across the Internet. Only rather than clicking, you'll be tapping or swiping.

This chapter discusses how to install the StumbleUpon app on your device, how to create an account and Stumble with the app, and describes the overall ways that you can best use StumbleUpon on your iPhone or iPad.

Installing the App

To use your StumbleUpon iPhone or iPad app, you first need to download or install the app from the App Store.

1. **From the Home screen of your device, click on the App Store Icon. (See Figure 4-1.)**

The App Store icon

Figure 4-1: The App Store icon on the desktop.

2. In the news screen that appears, click on the Search icon.
   (See Figure 4-2.)

Search

Figure 4-2: The Search icon.

3. Tap once in the Search field to bring up your keyboard.

4. Type in StumbleUpon and tap the screen to select the
   StumbleUpon app.

   The next screen you see (Figure 4-3) is what you'll use to
   actually download and install the app to your device.

5. Tap Install and the app will begin the download/installa-
   tion process.

Tap Install

Figure 4-3: The Install option on the Download screen.

6. **After the app is done downloading, either open the app from the Download screen (see Figure 4-4) or go back to your desktop and click on the app. (See Figure 4-5).**

Tap Open

Figure 4-4: The Open App option on the Download screen.

Figure 4-5: The StumbleUpon App on the Home screen.

Creating an Account

We're assuming that you've been a good boy or girl and have now downloaded the StumbleUpon app to your device and have clicked on the StumbleUpon icon to launch the app itself.

What you'll now see is a screen where you can either Sign Up for an account or Sign In to your existing StumbleUpon account. (See Figure 4-6.)

To sign up — creating a new account, in other words — click Sign Up and from here you can create an account via one of three different ways: (See Figure 4-7)

Figure 4-6: Initial Sign Up and Sign In screen.

- ✔ **Via Facebook:** This is the option that is recommended if you are already logged in to your Facebook account via your iPhone or iPad. Because StumbleUpon uses your existing Facebook information, automatically creating your account is very fast.

    If this sounds like a plan, with your StumbleUpon app open, just tap the Join with Facebook button and you'll be prompted to sign in to your Facebook account if you are not already signed in on that particular device. (See Figure 4-8.)

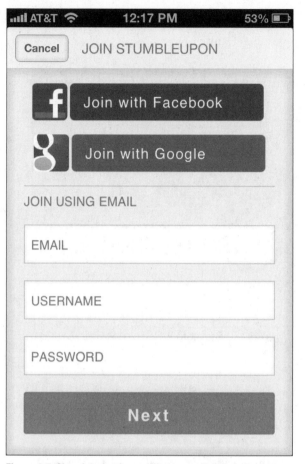

Figure 4-7: Showing the three different options for creating an account.

✔ **Via Email:** This option is for those people who don't have a Facebook account or simply don't want to link their Facebook and StumbleUpon accounts together. This option allows users to specifically identify the e-mail address, username, and password that they want for their new StumbleUpon account.

To get started, enter your email, username, and password under the section marked Join Using Email. (Refer to Figure 4-7).

✔ **Via Google:** For all you Google fans out there, just tap the Join with Google button (refer to Figure 4-7), enter your Gmail address and password in the new screen that appears (see Figure 4-9), tap Sign Up, and off you go to start Stumbling.

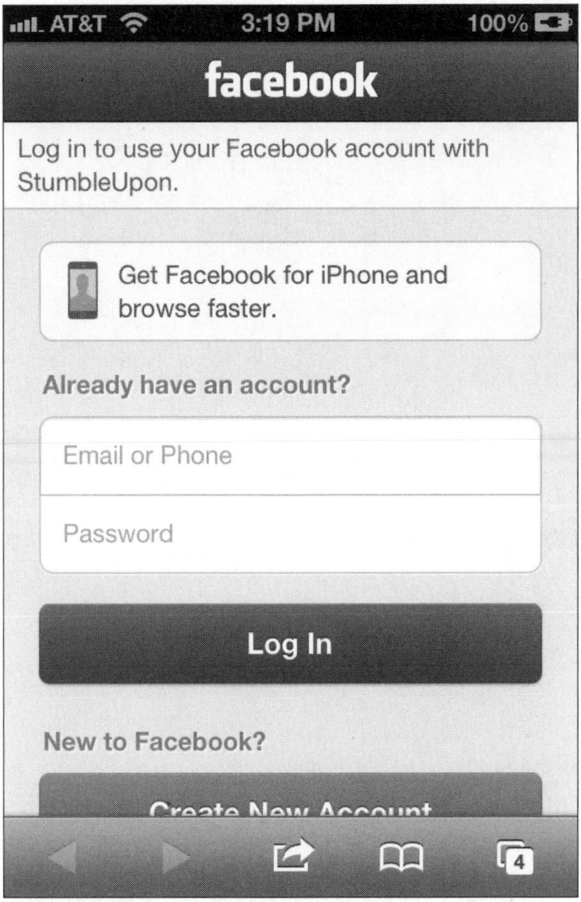

Figure 4-8: The Join with Facebook option.

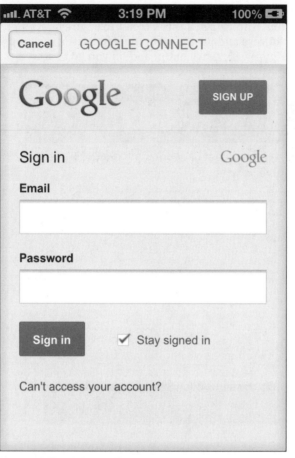

Figure 4-9: The Join with Google option.

Changing Your Profile Picture

Adhering to the policy of A Picture Is Worth a Thousand Words, StumbleUpon assumes that you want a profile picture linked to your account. Your initial profile picture is pretty generic — no, you won't recognize yourself because it's just a stupid placeholder — but changing that profile picture to something a bit more appropriate is so easy that, yes, even a caveman could do it. (Well, we can do it, and many people refer to us as cavemen.) Surely you can do it as well.

To change the picture on your profile:

1. **From the app's Home screen, tap the 3 horizontal lines in the upper-right corner. (See Figure 4-10.)**

2. **In the new menu screen that appears, tap the word Profile. (See Figure 4-11).**

Tap the lines ⌐

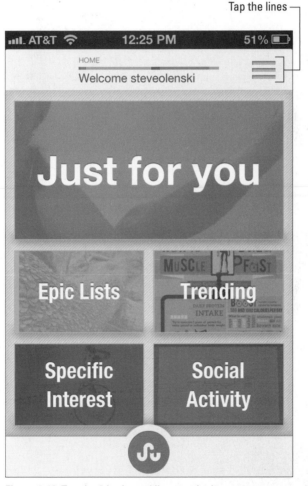

Figure 4-10: Tap the 3 horizontal lines on the home screen.

3. **Tap the picture currently displayed.**

   Unless StumbleUpon has been stalking you and taking your photo without your knowledge, the initial photo here will probably be one of those generic faceless models — not the handsome face you see in Figure 4-12.

Figure 4-11: The options that appear include Profile.

4. **In the new screen that appears (see Figure 4-13), choose whether you want to use an existing picture (Choose from Library) or go with a new picture (Take Photo).**

The Take Photo option is only for those who have a mobile device with a camera installed on it.

Figure 4-12: The current picture on your StumbleUpon account.

Figure 4-13: Options to choose a picture from the Library or take a new one.

Stumbling with the App

Okay, you have your account set up, and you have your new profile picture set as well. Time to start Stumbling!

Tap the StumbleUpon app icon on your device's Home screen to get to StumbleUpon's own Home screen.

From the Home screen (see Figure 4-14), you have five options to choose from:

✔ **Just for You:** Tap here to Stumble to websites that go across all your Interests.

✔ **Trending:** Tap here to see content that is very popular among all Stumblers.

✔ **Social Activity:** Tap here and you will see Stumbles that have been liked by those Stumblers you follow.

✔ **Specific Interest:** Tap here to select a specific Interest you'd like to Stumble.

✔ **Epic Lists:** Tap here to select from a group of four lists — Lists You'll Love, This Just In, Super Popular, and Lists You Follow. (See Figure 4-15.)

Figure 4-14: Desktop where you tap on the StumbleUpon app.

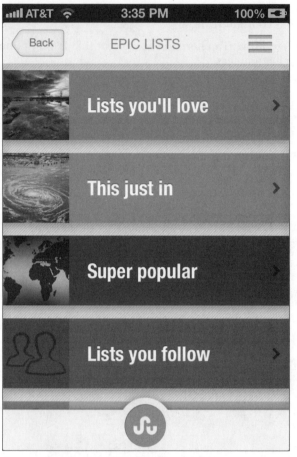

Figure 4-15: List of four Epic Lists options to choose from.

To Stumble to more content, you can either tap the Stumble button at the bottom of any web page you are on or swipe to the left.

Stumbling to a specific Interest

Stumbling to a specific Interest is very easy and is a great way to narrow your Stumbles to those Interests that, well, interest you. Here's what you do.

On your app's Home screen, tap the Specific Interest option to be taken to the Filter Interests page. (See Figure 4-16.) On this page, you'll see a list of all the specific Interests you're currently following. You'll also see Stumble modes at the top of the list — catchall categories that StumbleUpon came up with to get you on the fast lane to content. Your Stumble modes are as follows:

- ✔ **All Interests:** Tap here to Stumble all your Interests.

- ✔ **Trending**: Tap here to see the Stumbled content that is popular at that given moment among Stumblers.

- ✔ **Activity:** Tap here to Stumble those pages that have been liked by those Stumblers you are following.

- ✔ **Photos:** As you expect, tap here to Stumble only photographs.

- ✔ **Videos:** Same as above, only tapping here will take you to videos only.

- ✔ **News:** Tap here to get all the latest news.

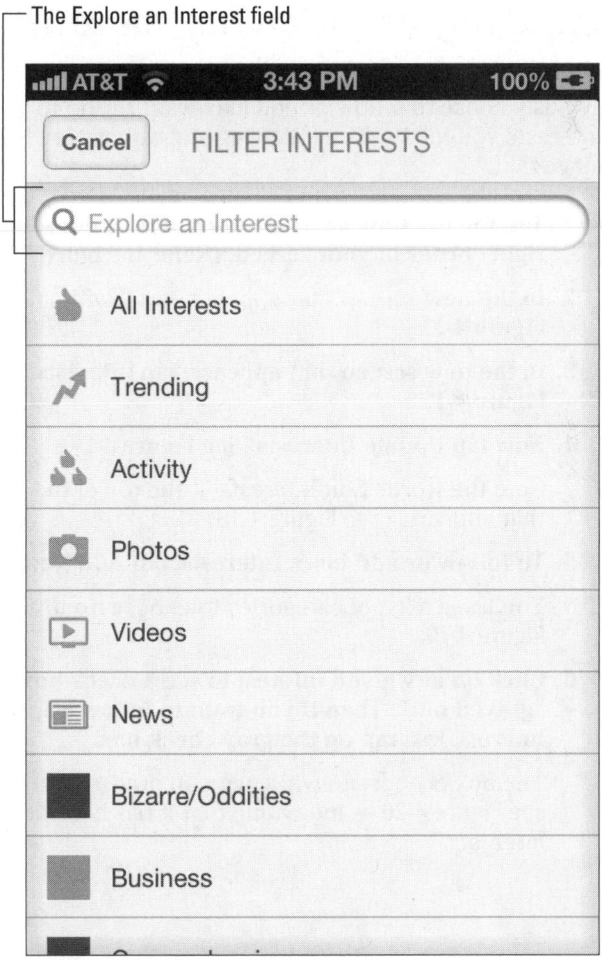

The Explore an Interest field

Figure 4-16: The Filter Interests screen.

You also have the option to explore an interest by typing in any interest you are not currently following in the appropriately named Explore an Interest field at the top of the screen (refer to Figure 4-16) and then tapping Search.

Scroll down to see more of your Interests below the Stumble modes.

After you're done exploring the web page you Stumbled upon, you can tap the 3 horizontal lines in the upper-right corner of the screen and then tap the Filter Interests option (refer to Figure 4-11) to take you back to the Filter Interests screen.

Removing or following more Interests

From time to time, you may either want to remove an interest you previously chose to follow or you may want to add to your list of Interests you follow. The following steps show you how to manage that:

1. **Tap the (by now familiar) horizontal 3 lines in the upper-right corner of your screen. (Refer to Figure 4-10.)**

2. **In the new screen that appears, tap Profile. (Refer to Figure 4-11.)**

3. **In the new screen that appears, tap Interests. (Refer to Figure 4-12.)**

4. **Now tap Update Interests (See Figure 4-17.)**

   Note the words Edit Interests at the top of the new screen that appears. (See Figure 4-18)

5. **To follow or add more Interests, tap Add New Interests.**

   You'll see a list of categories to choose from, as shown in Figure 4-19.

6. **Click on any given interest to see a check box that's "grayed out". Then if you want to follow a specific Interest, just tap on the gray check box.**

   The box changes to white with an orange background — see Figure 4-20 — indicating that it has been added to your Interests.

7. To remove or unfollow an interest, go back to the Edit Interests screen (refer to Figure 4-18) and then tap on the Interest you want to unfollow or remove and you will see that the check box is now gray. (See Figure 4-21).

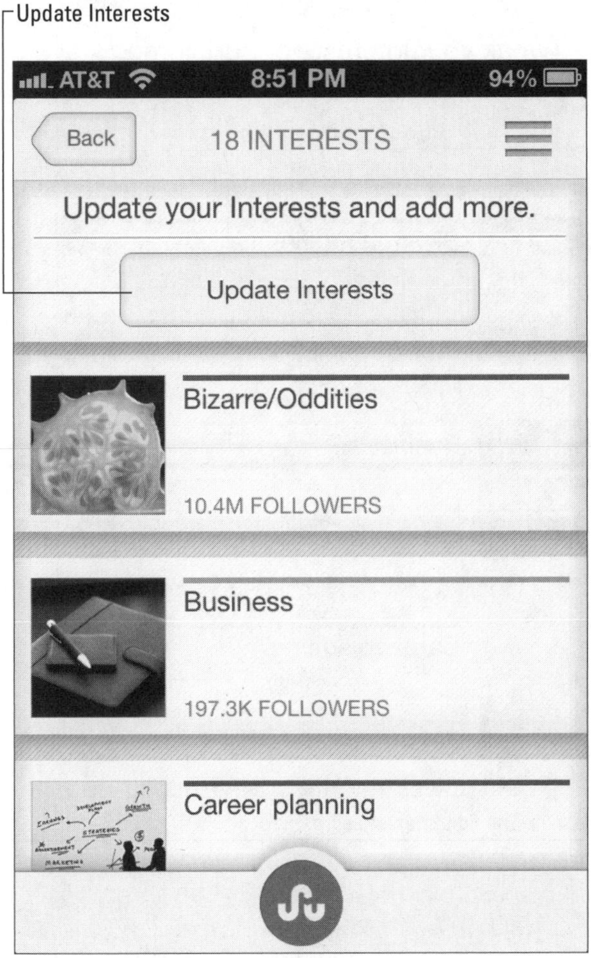

Figure 4-17: The Update Interests option.

Edit Interests

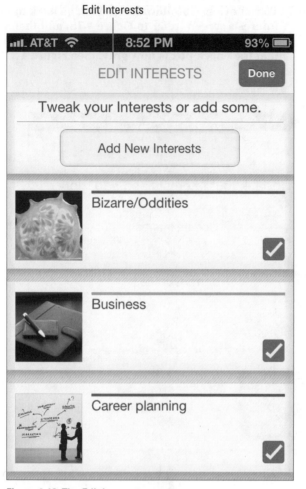

Figure 4-18: The Edit Interests screen.

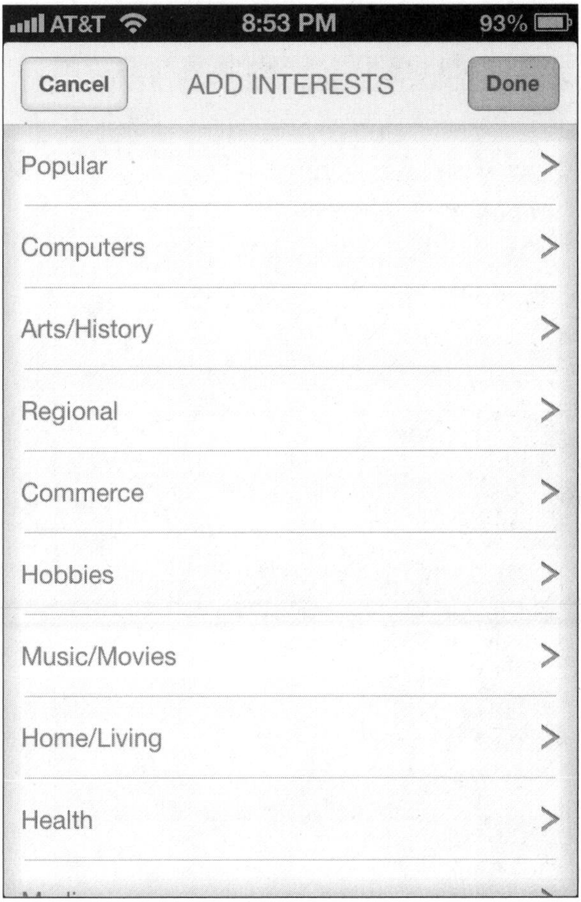

..ıll AT&T 📶	8:53 PM	93% 🔋

Cancel	ADD INTERESTS	Done

Popular　　　　　　　　　　　　　　　 >

Computers　　　　　　　　　　　　　　 >

Arts/History　　　　　　　　　　　　　 >

Regional　　　　　　　　　　　　　　　 >

Commerce　　　　　　　　　　　　　　 >

Hobbies　　　　　　　　　　　　　　　 >

Music/Movies　　　　　　　　　　　　 >

Home/Living　　　　　　　　　　　　　 >

Health　　　　　　　　　　　　　　　　 >

Figure 4-19: Your Add Interests categories.

Orange means you're following

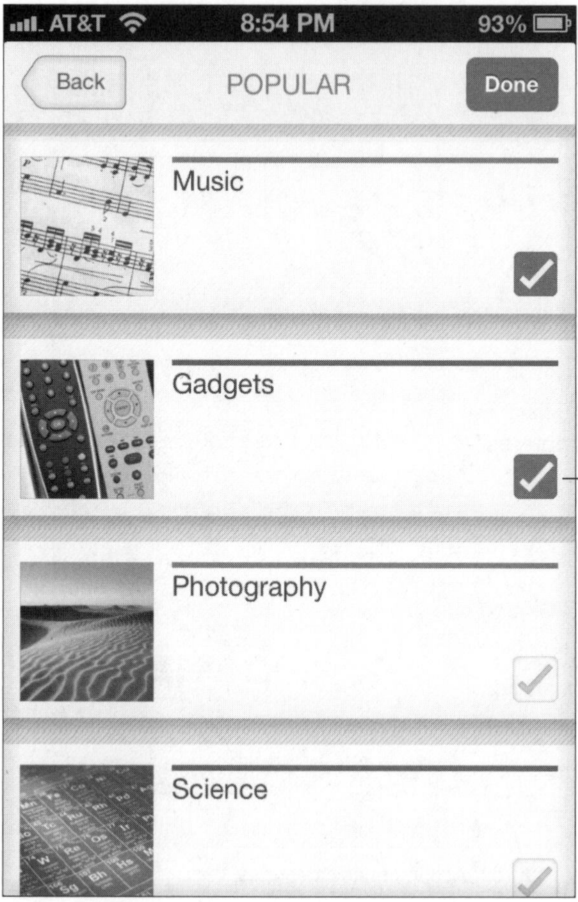

Figure 4-20: An orange background indicates an Interest you are now following.

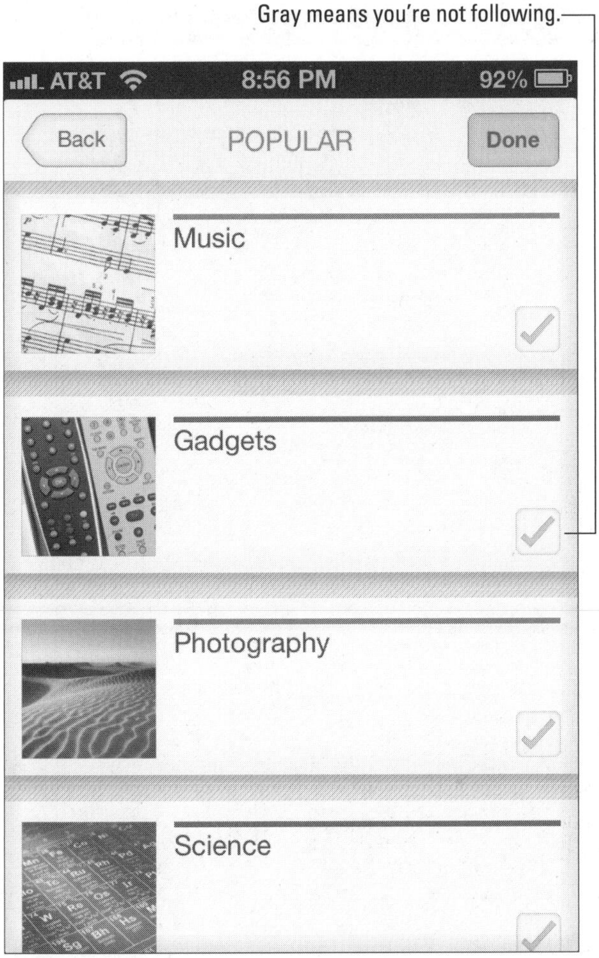

Gray means you're not following.

Figure 4-21: A gray check box shows an Interest you are no longer following.

Sharing a web page

Okay, so you've Stumbled upon a web page or website that you want to share. Great! This is social media, after all, and what's more social than sharing?

You have many ways to share a web page that you Stumbled upon. Start by tapping the Share button on the StumbleBar (located at the top of the screen on an iPad and the bottom of the screen on an iPhone — see Figure 4-22 — and you'll get a menu — see Figure 4-23) where you have the following options:

The Share button

Figure 4-22: The Share button.

✔ **Add To List:** You can create a list of Stumbled content that you can then make public (for anyone to see) or private (which can only be seen by those who follow you).

✔ **Email:** Add an e-mail address in the To field, add a message, click Send, and it's off. (See Figure 4-24.)

✔ **Another Stumbler:** Tapping this option lets you see a list of those Stumblers that you follow AND that are following you. (See Figure 4-25.)

From the list you can choose which fellow Stumbler you want to share this particular content with.

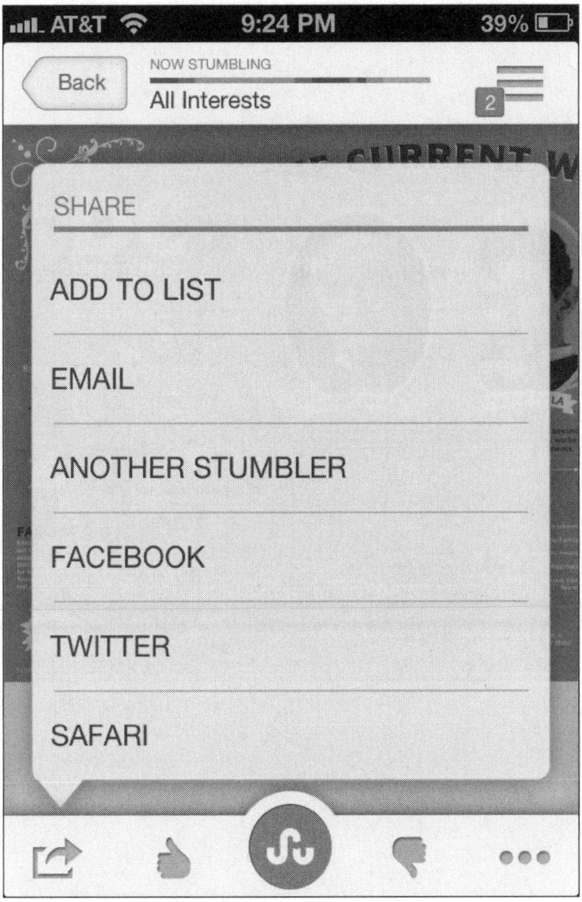

Figure 4-23: The Share options menu.

You do this by tapping on the gray check mark next to that individual's name and then tapping Next in the menu that appears.

After you tap Next, you're taken to a new screen (See Figure 4-26) where you see the title of the content, the original link, and whom you are sharing it with, along with a message box where you can include a personal message to the person you are sharing the content with.

To share a Stumble with a fellow Stumbler, you must first be following each other.

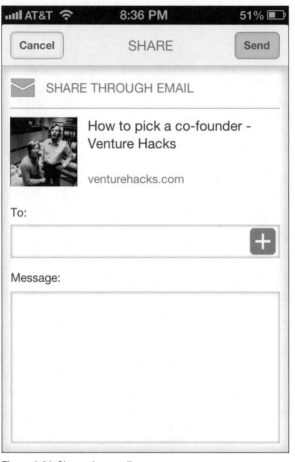

Figure 4-24: Share via e-mail screen.

✓ **Facebook:** When you tap this option, you are brought to a screen which, similar to the Share To Another Stumbler screen, contains the title of the content, along with the original link and a message box where you can include a personal message. (See Figure 4-27.)

When you're ready to share, tap Send and the stumbled content will be posted to your Facebook page

Figure 4-25: List of Stumblers you can share a stumble with.

Figure 4-26: The Share with a Fellow Stumbler screen.

✔ **Twitter:** Again, similar to the other Share options, when you tap this option, you are taken to a screen that contains the title of the content along with the original link and a message box where you can include a personal message. (See Figure 4-28.)

With Twitter, you are limited to 140 characters in your Tweet (message).

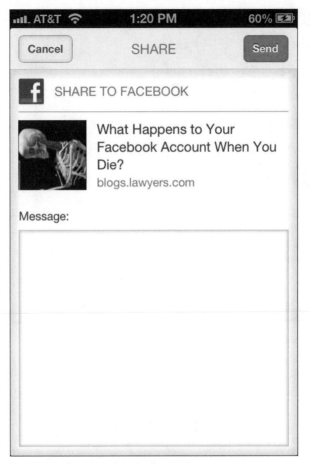

Figure 4-27: Share via Facebook screen.

Figure 4-28: Share via Twitter screen.

Liking or disliking a web page

Okay, so you've Stumbled upon a web page or website that you like and you want other Stumblers to know that you liked it.

You can "like" the page — in a social media sense — just by tapping the Thumbs Up icon. (See Figure 4-29.)

When you like a web page, the following occurs:

✔ The web page you liked will be added to your Profile Page, more specifically in a section entitled, appropriately enough, Likes. (Refer to Figure 4-12.)

✔ This section stores all the web pages you like for future reference — plus other Stumblers can view them as well.

✔ It alerts the folks at StumbleUpon as to what kind of content you want to see in the future.

✔ And finally, when you like a web page, it will be shared to your fellow Stumblers by showing up when they StumbleUpon new content.

Now, as for disliking a web page . . .

As you probably expect, instead of tapping that Thumbs Up icon to dislike a web page, you tap the Thumbs Down icon. (See Figure 4-29.)

When you dislike a web page, it lets the folks at StumbleUpon know what kind of content you don't like so they know not to include the same type of content in future Stumbles.

Additionally, you have the option to report a specific page to StumbleUpon.

To do this, tap those 3 dots you see at the bottom of the screen on the screen. (Again, see Figure 4-29.)

Doing so brings up a menu. (See Figure 4-30.) Tapping the Report An Issue menu item takes you to a new screen with 3 options, as shown in Figure 4-31. Your options are as follows:

✔ **Report As Spam:** Tap this option to report this particular web page as spam.

✔ **Seen Page Already:** Tapping this option lets StumbleUpon know that this particular web page is a page that you already Stumbled upon and you don't want to see this page again.

✔ **Page Does Not Load:** Just as the name implies, tapping this option lets StumbleUpon know that a particular web page did not load properly when you tried to view it.

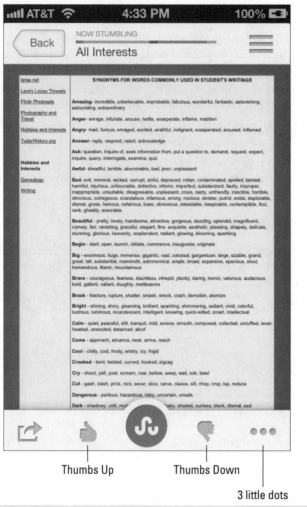

Thumbs Up

Thumbs Down

3 little dots

Figure 4-29: Thumbs Up icons, Thumbs Down icons, and 3 little dot icons.

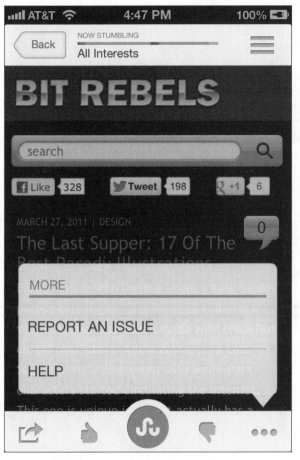

Figure 4-30: The More menu.

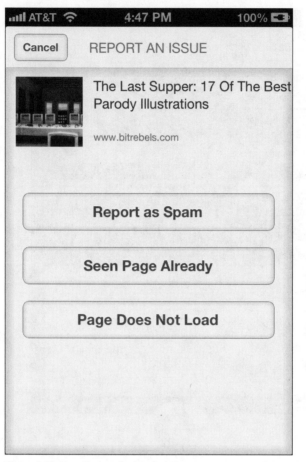

Figure 4-31: Your Report An Issue options.

Accessing your likes

Okay, so you've liked a whole bunch of web pages and websites and now you want to go back and see them all.

Lucky for you, all your Likes are kept for future reference.

To access your Likes, do the following:

1. **Go to your Profile screen.**

   See the "Changing Your Profile Picture" section, earlier in this chapter, for more on how to access your Profile screen.

2. **On your Profile screen, tap on the Likes option (refer to Figure 4-12).**

   A new screen appears, listing all the web pages you have liked previously. (See Figure 4-32.)

3. **Tap a Like entry to jump straight to that web page.**

   To review all your Likes, simply scroll down with your finger on the screen.

Figure 4-32: Your list of Likes.

Finding and following people you know on StumbleUpon

To find and follow people you know on StumbleUpon, start by going to your Profile screen. (Not sure how to do that? Check out the "Changing Your Profile Picture" section, earlier in this chapter.)

OK, on your Profile screen now? Just scroll down on the screen to see (a) the Following option and (b) the Followers option.

When you tap on Following or Followers, you have the following options:

- ✔ Scroll through to see all those Stumblers you are currently following.
- ✔ Find Friends.

The Find Friends option is what you want. When you tap on Find Friends, a new screen with 3 options greets you, as shown in Figure 4-33:

- ✔ **Scan My Address Book:** Tapping this option scans the address book on your device to see if anyone in your address book is also currently on StumbleUpon. You then have the option to follow them on StumbleUpon.

- ✔ **Find Facebook Friends:** Tapping this option brings up any of your Facebook friends who are also on StumbleUpon. You then have the option to follow them on StumbleUpon.

- ✔ **Find Twitter Friends:** Tapping this option brings you to a screen similar to Facebook, only this time it lists those you follow on Twitter who are also on StumbleUpon. You then have the option to follow them on StumbleUpon.

To find connections via Facebook and Twitter, you must first be signed in to these accounts.

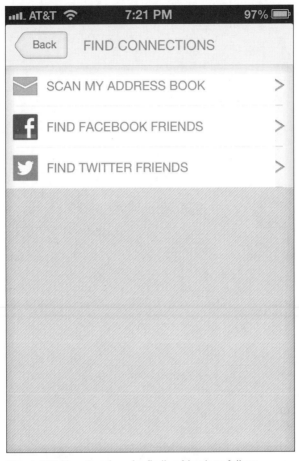

Figure 4-33: Your 3 options for finding friends to follow.

Chapter 5

Using StumbleUpon on Your Android Phone, Tablet, NOOK, or Kindle Fire

* *

In This Chapter

▶ Installing the StumbleUpon app on your device

▶ Using your app on an Android phone, a tablet, a NOOK or a Kindle Fire

▶ Stumbling your Interests

▶ Sharing your Stumbles

▶ Following folks who Stumble

▶ Finding out about permissions

▶ Accessing StumbleUpon's Help feature

* *

*I*t shouldn't surprise you that, because there's a StumbleUpon app for the iPhone and iPad, you'll also find one built just for the Android and its associated tablet, NOOK, and Kindle Fire devices. And much like the iPhone and iPad StumbleUpon app for those devices, the app for Android has also received rave reviews.

The editors at CNET.com had this to say about the Android version of the app: "StumbleUpon has clearly gone to great lengths to make the stumbling experience even simpler for its users." They also made reference to the Home screen, which "shows off more visually appealing thumbnails for each category."

Installing the App

The first thing you need to do is download and install the StumbleUpon app onto your device.

The following instructions show you how to download and install the app on a Kindle Fire device. Downloading and installing the app on other devices will be similar.

1. **From your Kindle Fire Home screen, tap Apps in the menu that runs across the top of the screen. (See Figure 5-1.)**

2. **In the new screen that appears, tap Store in he upper-right corner. (See Figure 5-2.)**

   You are brought to the Store screen for your Kindle Fire device.

Figure 5-1: The Kindle Fire Home screen.

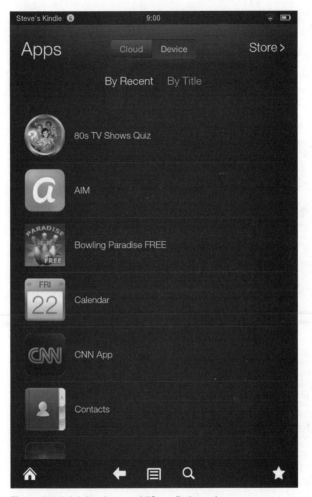

Figure 5-2: Look for the word "Store" along the top.

3. In the Search field at the top of the screen, type in StumbleUpon.

4. Tap StumbleUpon Kindle Fire in the Search Results listing. (See Figure 5-3.)

5. In the new screen that appears, tap on the StumbleUpon icon to start the installation process. (See Figure 5-4.)

Figure 5-3: The Store screen's Search field.

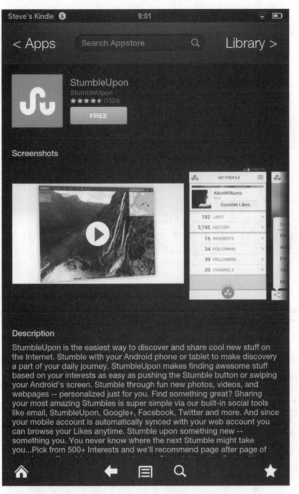

Figure 5-4: Tap the StumbleUpon App for Kindle Fire entry.

6. Tap the Get App button. (See Figure 5-5.)

7. Wait for the installation process to run its course and then tap Open to launch the app. (See Figure 5-6.)

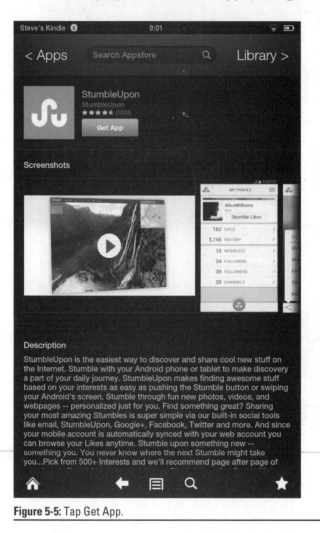

Figure 5-5: Tap Get App.

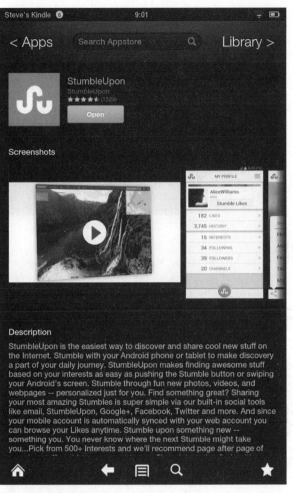

Figure 5-6: Tap Open.

Working with Your App

After you have downloaded and installed the StumbleUpon app onto your device, you're ready to start Stumbling — well, sort of.

First you have to either sign in to your existing StumbleUpon account or create a new account.

Tap on the StumbleUpon icon — right there on the "carousel" on your Kindle Fire — to start.

The first screen you come to after tapping the StumbleUpon icon is going to offer you the following two choices. (See Figure 5-7).

✔ Sign up for a StumbleUpon account.

✔ Sign in to your existing StumbleUpon account.

We discuss them one at a time.

The first option, signing up for a StumbleUpon account, offers three different ways to accomplish this. (See Figure 5-8).

✔ **By using your Facebook account:** This is the method of choice if you are already logged on to your Facebook account via your Android or other device. What's great about this method is that the registration for a StumbleUpon account goes a lot faster.

Why faster? Because StumbleUpon uses the information from your Facebook account to create an account automatically from that information. To confirm your new StumbleUpon account, you'll receive an e-mail from the folks at StumbleUpon that contains your login name and password.

✔ **Via e-mail:** If you choose this option, you'll use the provided boxes to identify which e-mail you want to use when creating your account, as well as specify what username and password you want to use on your StumbleUpon account.

This is the option to use if you (a) don't have a Facebook account or (b) want to keep your Facebook and StumbleUpon accounts separate.

✔ **By using the Google route:** Just tap the Google logo — you can't miss it — and then enter your Gmail e-mail and password.

You must have a Google account created for your device to use the Google option.

Figure 5-7: Your initial login screen.

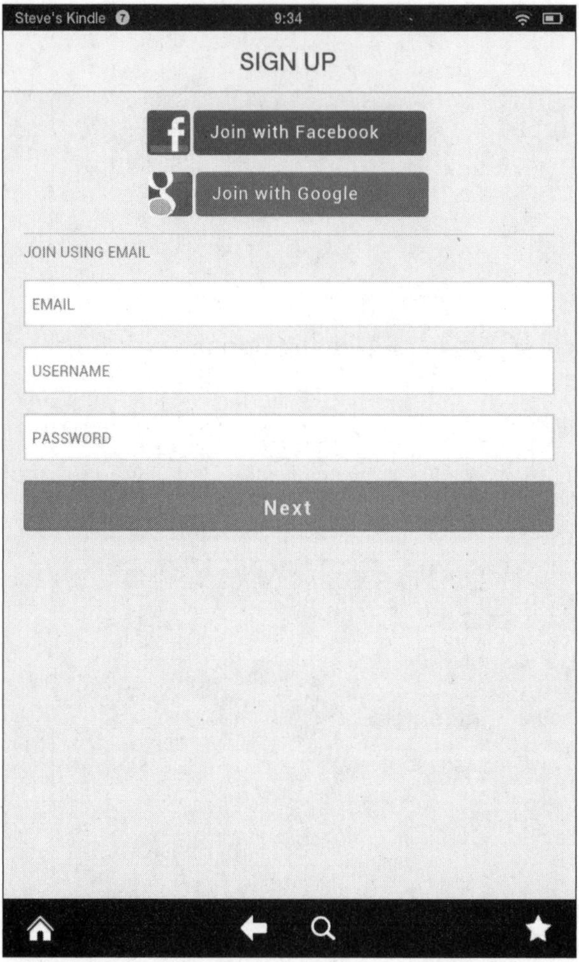

Figure 5-8: Three different ways to create a StumbleUpon account.

Changing your profile picture

Perhaps you want to change your profile picture. Fortunately, that step, unlike changing your driver's license photo, which you're stuck with for years, is a whole lot easier. And faster.

After you log in to your StumbleUpon account, here's all you do:

1. **Tap the Menu button at the upper right of the screen.**

   That's the three gray lines, one on top of another. (See Figure 5-9.)

   From here you'll see a drop-down menu of options, including Profile. (See Figure 5-10.)

The Menu button

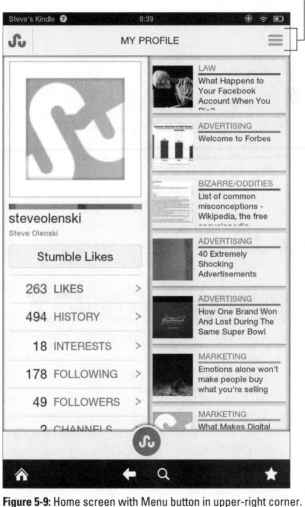

Figure 5-9: Home screen with Menu button in upper-right corner.

Figure 5-10: Drop-down menu with options, including Profile.

2. **On the menu that appears, tap Profile.**

   You'll be taken to the My Profile screen. (See Figure 5-11.)

3. **On the My Profile screen, tap your current picture — or, if you haven't added a picture yet, tap the placeholder image (the stylized SU).**

   Doing so brings up your options for uploading a new picture.

4. **Choose either Take Photo or From Library. (See Figure 5-12.)**

The Picture placeholder

Figure 5-11: The My Profile screen.

The From Library option is pretty straightforward. You use a dialog box to navigate through your hard drive until you find the photo you want to use for your profile picture

Choosing the Take Photo option is a bit more involved. First, your device's camera will open automatically — provided your device has a camera installed — and you have the option of zooming in or out before taking your photo. When you're ready, tap the blue circle at the bottom of the screen.

If you're happy with the picture you took, tap the check box at the bottom left of the screen. (See Figure 5-13.) That picture gets added to your StumbleUpon Profile.

However, if you're not happy with the picture you took, tap the X at the top left of the screen (again, see Figure 5-13.) and you'll be taken back to your Profile page. (From here, you need to start the process over again with Step 1 in the preceding list.

Make sure that your image is in landscape orientation as opposed to portrait orientation. If the image you want to use is in portrait orientation, it will load into StumbleUpon sideways regardless of how the image looks on your device in the first place.

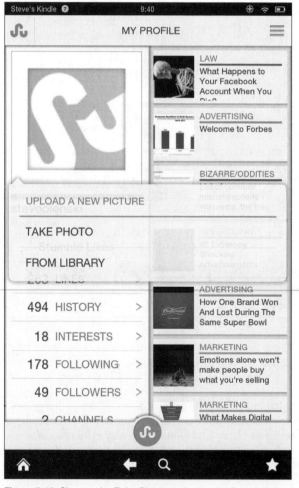

Figure 5-12: Choose the Take Photo option or the From Library option.

Tap here to reject image   Tap here to OK image

Figure 5-13: Approving or rejecting an image for Profile.

Stumbling with your StumbleUpon app

So you think you're ready to start Stumbling? Well, you're right, you are.

First, however, you need to make sure that you're on the StumbleUpon app's Home screen. If, say, you're still on the Profile screen after having changed your profile picture (see the preceding section), simply tap the StumbleUpon icon in the upper-left corner of the screen. (Refer to Figure 5-12.)

The StumbleUpon app's Home screen (see Figure 5-14) offers you multiple ways to start Stumbling to your heart's content:

- **Stumble Content Just for You:** Tapping this will take you to Stumbled content based on your personal settings.

  For example, if you're into movies, you'll see Stumbled content about movies. (See Figure 5-15.)

- **Stumble Lists:** Tap on Lists and you'll see five sublists — Lists You'll Love, This Just In, Super Popular, Lists You Follow, and Lists You've Created. As you tap each of these sublists, you'll see recommended lists from that category along the right hand side of the screen. (See Figure 5-16).

- **Stumble Trending:** Tapping this button takes you to popular pages — in fact, the most popular pages on all of StumbleUpon. Who decides what's popular? Why, the legions of Stumblers who decide to "like" them, that's who!

- **Stumble a Specific Interest:** Tap here and a new pop-up screen appears, offering you the following options. (See Figure 5-17.)

  - *Explore an interest,* where you set sail on the open seas and start exploring. Okay, maybe not the open seas but you will explore, literally. Just type in any interest in the Explore an Interest field and away you go!

  - *All Interests,* to Stumble all your specified Interests.

  - *Trending,* where you can also Stumble to content that is very popular among fellow Stumblers.

  - *Videos and Photos,* where you can Stumble either videos or photos related to your specific interest.

  - Plus at the bottom, you'll always see the list of your specific Interests — just pick one and Stumble in that particular direction. (To see all your Interests, you may need to scroll down a bit.)

- **Stumble Social Activity:** Tap here to see the Stumbles that have been liked by the people you're following on StumbleUpon. (For more on following, check out the "Finding and following people you know on StumbleUpon" section, later in this chapter.

The Menu button

Figure 5-14: The Home screen.

Figure 5-15: Seeing where Stumble Content leads you.

As of this writing, you weren't able to use the app itself to block videos from showing up in your Stumbles. However, you can always log on to www.stumbleupon.com via your device's/computer's browser and block videos from there.

Here's how to do that.

After you have logged on to your StumbleUpon account from your device or computer:

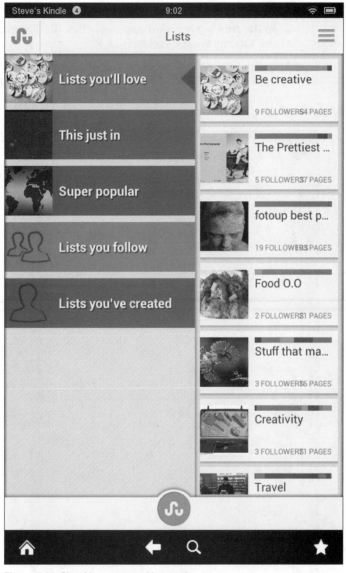

Figure 5-16: Checking out your Lists options.

1. **Click or tap on the down arrow next to your name at the top of the screen.**

   Doing so opens a menu with number of options — including a Settings option. (See Figure 5-18.)

2. **Click or tap Settings.**

3. **In the new screen that appears, click the Stumbles link in the top right. (See Figure 5-19.)**

4. **In the Content Filters section of the new screen that appears, deselect the box marked Video. (See Figure 5-20.)**

   Videos are now blocked from showing up in your Stumbles.

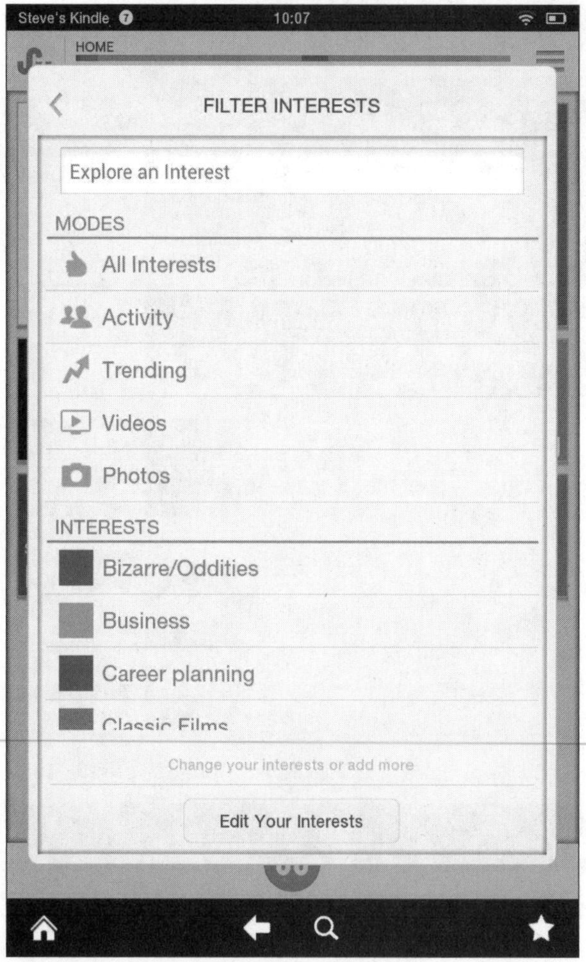

Figure 5-17: The Stumble an Interest screen.

Figure 5-18: The drop-down menu includes Settings option.

The Stumbles link

Figure 5-19: Look for the Stumbles link.

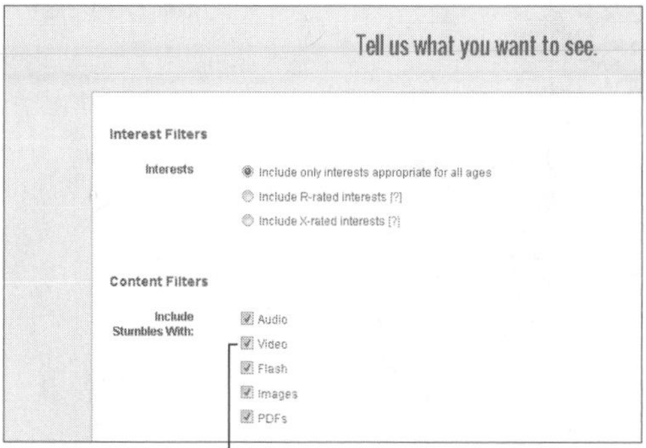

Tell us what you want to see.

Interest Filters

Interests

Content Filters

Deselect the Video check box.

Figure 5-20: To block videos, deselect the Videos check box.

Removing or following more Interests

Let's face it: Things change, right? With that being said, you may very well find yourself wanting to remove an interest you previously thought was worth following. On the other hand, you may find yourself wanting to now follow a new interest. How do you this? Piece of cake. Follow these steps:

1. **Tap the Menu button at the upper right of the screen.**

   That's the three gray lines one on top of another. (Refer to Figure 5-14.)

2. **On the menu that appears, tap Profile. (Refer to Figure 5-10.)**

   You are then taken to the My Profile screen.

3. **On the My Profile screen, tap Interests.**

   This brings up a side panel, as shown in Figure 5-21.

4. **Tap Edit Interests.**

   Doing so brings up a new window to manage your current Interests plus add new ones, as shown in Figure 5-22.

Figure 5-21: The Interests side panel.

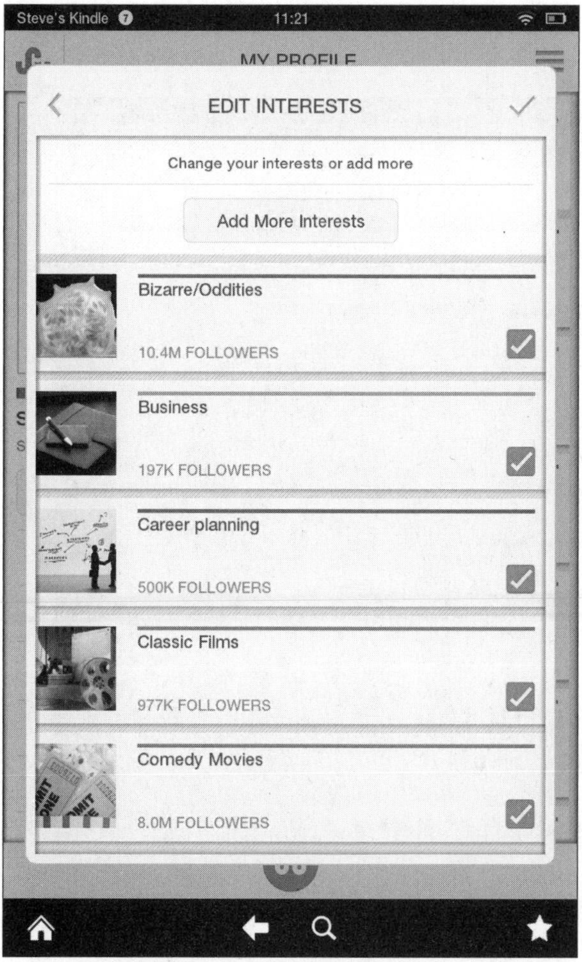

Figure 5-22: Manage your current Interests and add new ones.

5. **To remove a current interest, simply tap the interest to remove the check mark.**

6. **To add Interests, tap Add More Interests.**

   Doing so brings up a new window of options, as shown in Figure 5-23.

7. **From here, simply tap an interest you want to follow and tap each individual interest within that group.**

   The highlighted check mark denotes which new interest you're now following.

8. **To save your changes, tap the check mark at the upper right of the screen.**

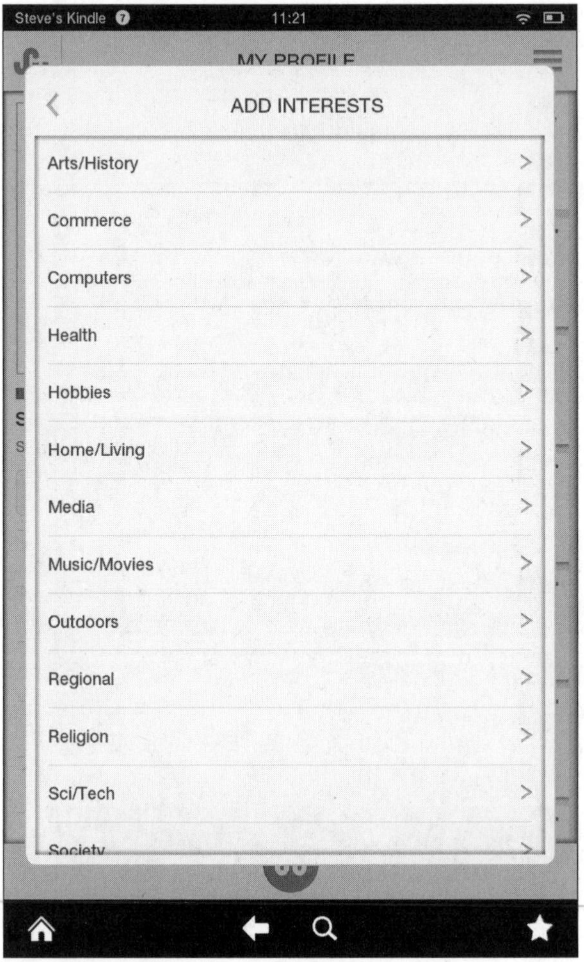

Figure 5-23: Your Add Interests choices.

Navigating on your Android device

When it comes to navigating on your Android device, you have a couple of different ways to manage that task by using the StumbleUpon app — and it all comes down to what it is you want to do.

One way is to use the Swipe method. To move on to your next Stumble, just swipe right to left across your touchscreen to move forward. (Tapping the StumbleUpon button achieves the same result, by the way.)

Swiping backward — or left to right on your touchscreen — takes you back to the screen you were just on. (Tapping the Back button or arrow accomplishes the same thing.)

Your next navigation option is to use the Menu button, the three gray lines at the upper right of the screen. By tapping the Menu button, you can access your profile, get help, view any pending shares other Stumblers have for you, sign out of the app, or exit the app. (You can also — via your Profile — access your Likes, Interests, History, Followers, and more, so the Menu button also acts as a great gateway to your content.)

Sharing a web page

Hey there, you just Stumbled upon a website you want to share with others. Fantastic! Fortunately, you have some great ways to do just that.

The first thing you want to do is tap the Share button, which is located at the lower left of the screen and looks kind of like the "less than" sign from your old math days. (Okay, it does have an extra three dots embedded on it, as Figure 5-24 makes clear, but let's not get caught up in the details.)

When you tap the Share button, you see five sharing options to choose from, as shown in Figure 5-25:

  ✔ **Email:** The Email option allows you to e-mail someone a link to this Stumbled content. Note that the e-mail itself will come from the StumbleUpon app and not from the e-mail account you have loaded on your device. (If you want to use your own e-mail account, check out "More Options," later in this list.)

  ✔ **Another Stumbler:** You can share this content with a fellow Stumbler. By sharing with another Stumbler you are telling your fellow Stumbler that you think they would enjoy this content.

  To share it with another Stumbler, however, you must each be following one other.

  ✔ **Facebook:** Tap this option to share the content on your Facebook Page.

  ✔ **Twitter:** Tap this option to — you guessed it — share the content via your Twitter account.

✔ **More Options:** Tapping this option brings up a menu with additional sharing options that are based on what apps you have on your device at the time, including an option for sending content via the e-mail client loaded on your device.

— The Share button

Figure 5-24: The Share button on the bottom left of the screen.

If your device of choice is a NOOK, be sure that you've set up your standard NOOK e-mail account first before you try to share a Stumble via an e-mail. If you don't do that necessary prep work first, you'll find yourself stuck on the e-mail setup page — an unwelcome state of affairs caused by a design flaw with the NOOK itself.

If you do find yourself stuck, don't panic. To remedy the situation, start by turning off your NOOK, which (of course) automatically signs you out of the StumbleUpon app. Then restart the NOOK and set up your NOOK e-mail *before* launching your StumbleUpon app.

Figure 5-25: The five sharing options.

Liking a web page

Okay, raise your hand if you know who Fonzie was. If you're too young to remember, go ask someone over the age of, say, 35 or 40.

Fonzie was a TV character who gave his approval of something with the aid of a (truly hip) thumbs-up sign. If he liked something, you knew that the thumbs-up gesture would soon make an appearance. It's the same thing with StumbleUpon.

When you come across a Stumble or web page you like, just tap the Thumbs Up button at the bottom of the screen. (See Figure 5-26.) That's all there is to it. Tap the Thumbs Up button and you're your own Fonzie.

Thumbs Up!

Figure 5-26: The Thumbs Up button.

Accessing your Likes

So you have all these *Likes* — the websites you've identified as ones you like with the help of the Thumbs Up button. And now, you want to go back and look at them. You want to see all these great websites you've (for all intents and purposes) *bookmarked* StumbleUpon-style.

To access your Likes, just go to your My Profile screen.

To get to your My Profile screen:

1. **Tap the three horizontal lines at the top right of the screen. (Refer to Figure 5-9.)**
2. **From the Menu that appears tap Profile.**

From here, you can do one of the following:

✔ Tap the Likes item in the menu under your profile picture (see Figure 5-27) and then scroll through each and every one of your Likes.

✔ Stumble through previous Likes by tapping the Stumble Likes button right below your profile picture. (Again, see Figure 5-27.)

Adding a web page to StumbleUpon

Unfortunately, you currently don't have a way to add a new website to StumbleUpon's official index of sites by using the app. However, if you do want to add a website, you can still do that via the standard StumbleUpon website www. stumbleupon.com.

Using the browser on your device, log on to StumbleUpon.com. Then just follow the same steps as if you were adding a web page on your computer.

For more help on adding a website, visit http://help.stumbleupon.com.

For more information on using the StumbleUpon website, please refer to Chapter 2.

The Stumble Likes button

The Likes item

Figure 5-27: Accessing your likes on your My Profile screen.

Finding and following people you know on StumbleUpon

When you make the decision to "follow" someone on StumbleUpon, you're telling that person that you like the kind of content that he or she Stumbles. And as a direct result of your "following" him or her, whatever Likes he or she has tagged appear automatically in your StumbleUpon stream.

Finding and following someone you know on StumbleUpon is pretty easy. Like pretty much everything else on StumbleUpon, you have multiple paths you can follow when you want to "follow," as spelled out in the following list:

1. **Start by tapping the Menu button at the upper-right corner of your app window to access your profile. (Refer to Figure 5-9.)**

2. **On the menu that appears, tap Profile.**

3. **Tap either the Following option or the Followers option.**

   It doesn't matter which one. Whichever option you choose, you'll be greeted by a new screen similar to what you see in Figure 5-28.

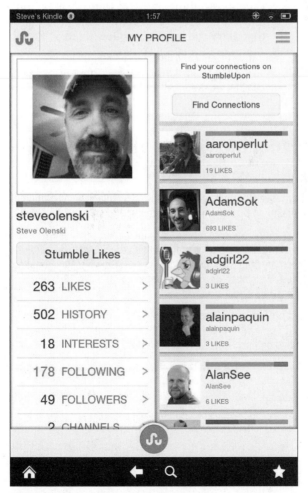

Figure 5-28: The Find Connections screen.

4. **Tap Find Connections at the top of this new screen.**

Yet another new screen appears with three options, as shown in Figure 5-29:

- **Scan My Address Book**: Tapping this item scans the address book on your device to see if anyone in your address book is also currently on StumbleUpon. You then have the option to follow them on StumbleUpon.

- **Find Facebook Friends:** Tapping this item brings up any of your Facebook friends who are also on StumbleUpon. You then have the option to follow them on StumbleUpon.

- **Find Twitter Friends**: Tapping this item brings you to a screen similar to what appears when you choose the Facebook option, only this time it will be those you follow on Twitter who are also on StumbleUpon. You then have the option to follow them on StumbleUpon.

You must first be logged in to Facebook and Twitter on your device to find and follow connections via these social media networks.

Sending messages via StumbleUpon to another Stumbler

Sadly, you can't send a message to another Stumbler via the StumbleUpon app. But that doesn't mean that all lines of communication are cut off. On the contrary.

You can still communicate with another Stumbler. All you do is type out a message when you are sharing a particular website with the person you want to communicate with. When the other Stumbler receives your Stumble, the message you typed will be included. (For more on sharing websites, see the "Sharing a web page" section, earlier in this chapter.)

In fact, you can hold entire conversations with someone via this method. Just remember that you and the person you want to engage in a conversation with need to be following each other.

You have one other way to follow a Stumbler: Simply visit his or her My Profile screen and slide the Following option slider to On, as shown in Figure 5-30.

To visit someone's My Profile screen, just tap on their image or name under Find Connections in your own My Profile screen. (Refer to Figure 5-28.).

Figure 5-29: Your Find Connections options.

The Following slider

Figure 5-30: The Following slider used to follow a Stumbler.

Reporting or blocking a web page

Back in the "Liking a web page" section, earlier in this chapter, we introduced you to Fonzie (also known as The Fonz) and his habit of giving something a thumbs-up gesture if he liked it. You'll never guess what he used to do if he *didn't* like something.

You got it. He would give it a thumbs down, and that's exactly what you can do via StumbleUpon when you come across a website you don't like and/or want to report.

The folks at StumbleUpon do their best to ensure that you only see the highest-quality content when you Stumble, but hey, they're human and mistakes can happen.

When the rare mistake occurs, they need your help to tell them about it. If you've Stumbled upon a website that you consider to be of poor quality, just tap the Thumbs Down button near the lower right on your screen to let the StumbleUpon folks know that they have to step up their game.

If you have more specific objections to the content that your app has served up, tap the More button — the button with the three dots stacked on top of one another at the lower (far) right of the screen. Doing so brings up a new screen where you have an option to reload the page — assuming that you had some problem with the original connection — or the option of reporting an issue. Tap the Report an Issue option to move on to a new screen with the three options shown in Figure 5-31.

> ✔ **Report as Spam:** Anytime you Stumble upon a web page or website that is spammy, illegal, or deceptive in nature, StumbleUpon wants to know about it. Tapping this button alerts the StumbleUpon Quality and Community Support teams.

> Any website that "just happens" to ask you to provide personal details such as your Social Security number, banking information, and so on, is definitely up to no good and should be reported Immediately.

> ✔ **Seen Page Already:** Just as the name implies, you've Stumbled upon a web page or website you've already seen before and really don't want to see it again.

> ✔ **Unable to Load Page:** If the web page or website you're trying to access will not load properly or does not load at all — Oh no! Not the dreaded "404 Error" message! — you can let StumbleUpon in on the bad news by tapping this option.

For more on reporting a bad web page, visit www.stumbleupon. com. In the search box at the top, type **report bad web page** and tap Enter.

Figure 5-31: Report an issue screen.

Asking for Location (And Other) Information

First and foremost, it is important to know that StumbleUpon takes the privacy of your information very seriously. It will never sell it or reveal it to any third-party companies.

At times, however, StumbleUpon will ask for permissions and location information as it relates to the Android app.

Here are the permissions that StumbleUpon will ask of you when using the StumbleUpon app and the reasoning behind such requests:

- ✔ **Location:** StumbleUpon will ask permission to access your approximate location. The reasoning here is that StumbleUpon can then use your location to provide you with recommendations such as nearby restaurants or stores that are based on your particular location. StumbleUpon will rarely access this information, and it does not track or store it at any time.

  You know that this information is being accessed when you see the Location icon appearing in the top navigation bar.

- ✔ **Personal contact information:** When you want to find fellow Stumblers from the address book loaded on your device, StumbleUpon will need to access your contact information to do so. If you don't give your permission, StumbleUpon won't be able to track down potential Stumblers among your contacts. It's as simple as that.

- ✔ **Network information:** A very important part of the StumbleUpon experience revolves around StumbleUpon's ability to use your network connection to access the websites it recommends in the first place. This permission allows StumbleUpon to do just that.

  Another important permission has to do with wireless connections. By allowing StumbleUpon to use your wireless connection, you help ensure that you won't lose connection to StumbleUpon if and when your device loses an over-the-air connection (a connection accessed on a phone without the need for a USB cable) but a wireless connection is present.

- ✔ **Storage:** When you go to another Stumble, StumbleUpon is behind the scenes loading the next Stumble so that it's ready when you are. The Storage permission allows StumbleUpon to always make sure that your next Stumble is always ready.

- ✔ **Device ID:** Quite simply, the Device ID permission allows StumbleUpon to connect your phone or device to your StumbleUpon account. It also gives StumbleUpon the opportunity to provide customer service and technical support. Additionally, it helps stop spammers who try and set up multiple accounts from the same device.

- ✔ **System tools:** Several permissions fall under this heading:

  - *Apps:* With this permission, you give StumbleUpon the right to look at the apps you've Stumbled and then generate more personalized app suggestions.

    The first time you Stumble apps, StumbleUpon will remind you about this permission with a message.

- *Share notifications:* With this permission, you allow StumbleUpon to send you a notification when another Stumbler has shared a website or Stumble with you.

- *Wallpaper:* With this permission, you're able to save an image that you Stumble as the wallpaper on your device.

✔ **Hardware controls:** This permission, which can be personalized via your device's General settings, provides flash and vibration alerts to be sent when you get a share Stumble from another Stumbler.

✔ **Near Field Communications (NFC):** The Android has a cool feature called the Beam that uses Near Field Communications technology to share information when devices are placed next to one another. With this permission, you're saying that it's okay to use this technology to share Stumbles between NFC-enabled phones.

For Beam to work, you must be running the Android 4.0 Ice Cream Sandwich OS at a minimum, and both devices must be NFC-enabled.

✔ **Google sign-in:** StumbleUpon account holders can sign in or sign up for a new account via their Google account. This permission allows this to occur.

Finding Helpful Tips

Tips are always a good thing, and from time to time, you may want to take advantage of the helpful tips StumbleUpon makes available to you.

To do so, follow these steps:

1. **Tap the StumbleUpon SU logo in the upper-left corner of your screen.**

   Doing so brings up the Home screen.

2. **Tap the Menu button — the three vertical lines at the upper right of the screen.**

3. **On the menu that appears, tap Help.**

   A new screen appears, displaying the following five options, as shown in Figure 5-32:

   - Rate the StumbleUpon app

   - Tour all the new features of the app

- Visit the Help Center
- View the StumbleUpon privacy policy
- View StumbleUpon's Terms of Service

When you tap any of the options (except for the second one), you are taken to an external link via the web browser installed on your device, where you are presented with tones of helpful information. The second option — the Tour one — stays within your StumbleUpon app as it gives you the guided tour of its features.

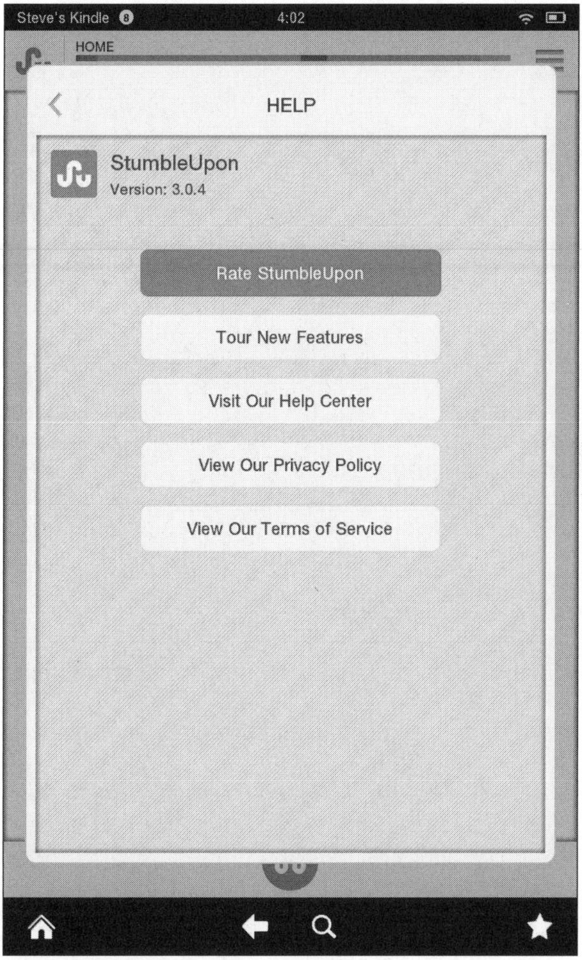

Figure 5-32: The Help screen options.

Chapter 6

Using StumbleUpon in Windows 8

*M*icrosoft has been around forever (at least in technology terms) and has dominated the desktop operating system market at the same time. If you're a PC user, you've been doing Windows for quite a while. Windows 8, however, is a radically different user experience than previous versions. For one, applications are dynamic, meaning that they update you whenever new content is added. (For you Apple lovers out there, this is the same idea as getting a notification when you get an update from applications.)

Given StumbleUpon's own dynamic nature, what better way to use Windows 8 than with a StumbleUpon app?

In this chapter, you find out how to install the StumbleUpon app in Windows 8, create and edit your profile, and of course, use the app in Windows 8.

With this chapter under your belt, you'll be all set to discover new content with the latest Microsoft operating system.

Installing the StumbleUpon App in Windows 8

First things first: If you're wavering about making that jump to Windows 8, we're here to tell you that the upgrade is definitely well worth it. Tasks function ten times faster than in Windows 7, and the user interface is slick with more app functionality.

My favorite aspect of Windows 8 is the ability to pick your favorite applications so that they show front and center on your Home screen — called the *Start screen* in Windows 8 terminology. Figure 6-1 gives you a sense of how that ability to customize the layout means that the look and feel of Windows 8 are completely different from prior Windows versions.

Figure 6-1: The Windows 8 layout provides a more customized experience, with only the important applications front and center.

Now that you have a sense of what the Start screen looks like, it's time to take you through the process of installing the StumbleUpon app on your Windows 8 device so that you can enjoy easy content discovery directly from your computer or Windows phone. Follow these steps to install the StumbleUpon app:

1. **Click the Store icon on the Start screen.**

   By default, the button is green.

2. **On the new screen that appears — the Store screen — scroll over until you reach the Social section.**

   You find a handy scroll bar at the bottom of the screen.

3. **Locate the icon for the StumbleUpon app in the Social section and then click it.**

   If you don't see the StumbleUpon app as one of the first three options, click the Top Free button; then scroll to the right until you find the StumbleUpon app.

4. **On the new screen that appears, click the Install button. (See Figure 6-2.)**

You have to wait a couple of minutes while the StumbleUpon app installs. Don't worry; it doesn't take too long. After the app is finished installing, you receive a green notification at the top right of your screen.

5. **Click the notification to open the StumbleUpon app.**

   If the notification itself disappears, don't worry. The app proper is now on your Start screen, as shown in Figure 6-3.

Okay, now you are ready to dive into the app. Click the StumbleUpon icon on your Start screen. The next screen takes you through a small tutorial; click the small black arrows on the right side of the screen to navigate the tutorial. After using the tutorial, you can either sign up for StumbleUpon or sign in to your current account. (If you read all the previous chapters, we hope that you have an account by now. If not, refer to Chapter 2.)

After you sign in, the StumbleUpon app immediately knows your name (of course it does, because you provided your name during the sign-up process, unless you called yourself "Dragon Lord"). Once again, you are taken through a tour to get accustomed to the Windows 8 app. Click the small black arrow to take the tour when prompted. When the tour ends, click the orange Start Stumbling button.

Figure 6-3: After you install the StumbleUpon app in Windows 8, it will show up on your Start screen for easy access to content discovery.

Using the App

Now that the Windows 8 StumbleUpon app is installed, you'll want to get used to browsing and sharing content. Multiple functions are unique to the Windows 8 environment. By the end of this chapter, you will know the ins and outs of these functions.

Scrolling or menu?

On the Home screen of the StumbleUpon app, you can browse several sections. Unlike the web browser version of StumbleUpon, however, you don't have navigation menus to choose from. Instead, you'll want to use the scroll bar at the bottom of the screen. To move to the different sections within the app, scroll to the right, as shown in Figure 6-4.

You can also choose a section from the Home screen by clicking the drop-down arrow at the upper left of the screen, as shown in Figure 6-5. Click the menu item to navigate to that section of the StumbleUpon app.

Figure 6-4: Use the scroll bar to view the different sections on the StumbleUpon app Home screen.

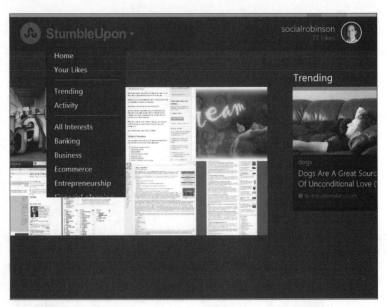

Figure 6-5: Click the drop-down arrow to choose the section you want to navigate to within the StumbleUpon app.

Stumbling

The next task is unique to Windows 8 in that, to Stumble, you either have to right-click your mouse or swipe at the bottom of the screen on a Windows phone. We assume that you're using a computer right now. Right-click, and you see a menu that allows you to either edit Interests or Stumble. Click Stumble. (See Figure 6-6.)

After clicking Stumble, you're taken to a piece of random content that StumbleUpon thinks you'll find interesting — just like every other Stumble, in other words. Go ahead and read, watch, or listen to the piece of content.

Figure 6-6: Right-click or swipe to see your options.

Liking and disliking content

Now that you've read, watched, or listened to that brilliant (or not-so-brilliant) piece of content, you have the option to "like" or "dislike" it. At first, the content is front and center, without any distractions. After you decide that you like or hate the content, either right-click your mouse or swipe at the top or bottom of the screen on your Windows phone. A black menu appears at the bottom of the screen with the options to like, dislike, or Stumble, as shown in Figure 6-7.

Perhaps you find the content interesting. Click the Like button and you see the button turn white. (To undo this action, simply click the button again and it will turn back to the original color.) The same holds true if you click Dislike.

This dog frequently rides a street car in the Russian city of Yekaterinburg, always getting on and off at the same stop.

Like   Dislike   Stumble

Figure 6-7: Options to like, dislike, or Stumble while on a piece of content.

Navigation

This section will be short and sweet. Consider that you've already liked or disliked a piece of content and want to go back to the main StumbleUpon app screen or maybe to some previous Stumbles. All you have to do is right-click (while on your computer) or swipe (at the top or bottom of your Windows phone). As shown in Figure 6-8, doing so brings up a menu at the top of the screen, which shows the title of the piece of content and an arrow pointing to the left.

To navigate back to the Home screen or previous Stumbles, click the white arrow and you're done.

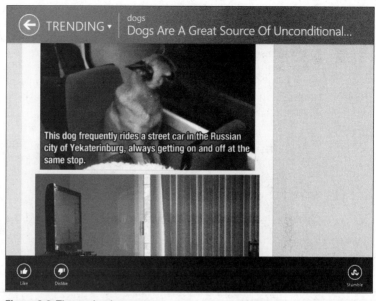

Figure 6-8: The navigation menu.

Sharing content with others

What if you want to share content with other people by e-mail or on StumbleUpon when using the Windows 8 app? No problem.

If you're using a computer, this particular trick is probably something you've never had to do before, so stay with me. Press and hold down the Windows key on your keyboard. It is the key directly to the left of Alt (which is on the left side of the spacebar). While holding down the Windows key, press the H key. Hold down both keys until you see a blue menu appear on the right side of your screen, as shown in Figure 6-9.

You see two options:

- ✔ StumbleUpon
- ✔ Mail

To share the piece of content with individual StumbleUpon users, click the StumbleUpon option on the blue menu on the right side of the screen. You then have the option to send a personalized note to the person/people you're sharing with. Make sure to choose the person/people that you want to share with first because you can't send the piece of content unless you click the profiles of the people you want to share with. If you're satisfied with your message, click Send and you're done.

Figure 6-9: The Share menu on the right side of the StumbleUpon app.

To send a piece of content by e-mail, click the Mail button on the blue menu. You're greeted by a screen similar to what you see in Figure 6-10, where you simply fill in the e-mail address that you want to send the piece of content to, add a personal message (if desired), and then click the Send button — the button with the blue fill that's directly to the right of the e-mail address in Figure 6-10.

Figure 6-10: Fill in an e-mail address, add a personal message, and then click Send.

Accessing past Likes

If you're the kind of person who uses StumbleUpon to archive content, you can use the Windows 8 StumbleUpon app to access content that you've previously liked. It's fairly easy. In fact, you can access your historical Likes in two easy ways.

One way is to scroll to the right on the StumbleUpon Home screen. You see a section for Likes at the far right. The other way is to use the drop-down menu at the upper left of every page. The menu turns different colors depending on what section you are in. All you have to do is click the drop-down menu's arrow and then choose Your Likes, which is the second item. (See Figure 6-11.)

Figure 6-11: Choose Your Likes to navigate to your past Likes.

The lazy scroll

We call this feature the lazy scroll because it allows you to jump right to a section if you don't feel like scrolling all the way to the right. If you want to jump straight to any of these four sections — Just for you, Activity, Trending, or Likes — this feature might resonate with you.

To jump to one of these four options, click the minus sign directly above the right arrow of the scroll bar, as shown in Figure 6-12. (*Note:* The minus sign turns white when your mouse cursor hovers over it, so this is reflected in Figure 6-12.)

After you click the minus sign, you see four boxes in the center of the screen. (Each box represents one of the four options mentioned here.) Click the box that corresponds to where you want to go.

Figure 6-12: Click the minus sign to be taken to a consolidated view of the four main sections of the Windows 8 StumbleUpon app.

Editing your StumbleUpon Interests

Perhaps you have a newfound love for racquetball and you want to find out more about how to become an expert player. Naturally, you need to consume as much content as possible before you hit the courts against the expert players, right?

With the StumbleUpon Windows 8 app, it's very easy to edit your Interests. When you're on the Home screen of the StumbleUpon app, right-click (with your mouse) or swipe (at the top or bottom on your Windows phone). Then click the Edit Interests button that appears at the bottom of your screen. (It's that circle icon with a pencil in the middle.) Next, you're presented with a list of Interests that are available in the StumbleUpon community. Choose which Interests to add and/or subtract. (Note that added Interests sport a check mark, as shown in Figure 6-13.)

When you're satisfied with the edits, click the orange Save Interests button at the bottom of the screen. *Voilà!* You're done.

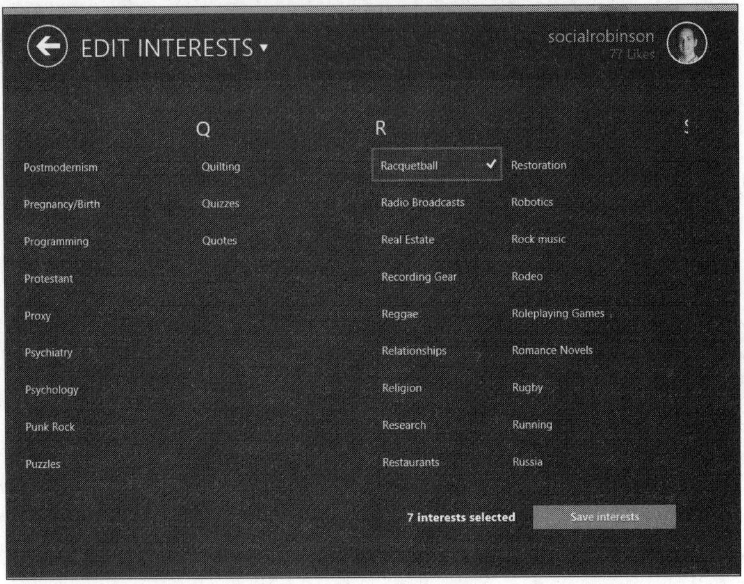

EDIT INTERESTS ▾   socialrobinson
                                                    77 Likes

	Q	R	
Postmodernism	Quilting	Racquetball ✔	Restoration
Pregnancy/Birth	Quizzes	Radio Broadcasts	Robotics
Programming	Quotes	Real Estate	Rock music
Protestant		Recording Gear	Rodeo
Proxy		Reggae	Roleplaying Games
Psychiatry		Relationships	Romance Novels
Psychology		Religion	Rugby
Punk Rock		Research	Running
Puzzles		Restaurants	Russia

7 interests selected   Save Interests

Figure 6-13: Pick the Interests that you want to add and/or subtract, and then click Save Interests.

After reading this chapter, you now have a step-by-step guide on how to install and use the StumbleUpon app for Windows 8. Microsoft's new operating system is designed for the 21st century, so take advantage of it. Now go find some great content to share with the community!

Chapter 7

Sharing Your Discoveries and Content

- -

In This Chapter

▶ Sharing your StumbleUpon content with your Stumbler friends

▶ Sharing across other social media platforms

▶ Viewing content from other Stumblers

▶ Blocking content from other Stumblers

- -

*R*emember the age-old adage "share and share alike"? Of course you do. Sharing is something we all learned to do as children, and in this chapter, we show you all the wonderful ways that you can share your StumbleUpon content. We also show you how not all sharing is good sharing.

Before jumping into all this sharing fun, it's worth noting that this chapter deals with sharing Stumbled content the old-fashioned way via the StumbleUpon website — www.stumbleupon.com. For information on sharing via a mobile device and app please refer to Chapters 4 and 5.

Sharing with Your StumbleUpon Friends

Okay, so you've come across this wickedly cool website featuring the latest and greatest music videos or recipes for borscht or something else that's unusual.

Being the good person you are, the first thing you think of is the good of others — in this case, the good of your fellow Stumblers. You want to tell them all about this way-cool site — which in the StumbleUpon world means that you want to "share" the site with them.

In a StumbleUpon context, you can only share content with someone you are following and with someone who is following you.

To do this sharing business, follow these steps:

1. **Click the Share icon at the top left of the screen. (See
   Figure 7-1.)**

   You'll find a Share icon on the StumbleBar as well.

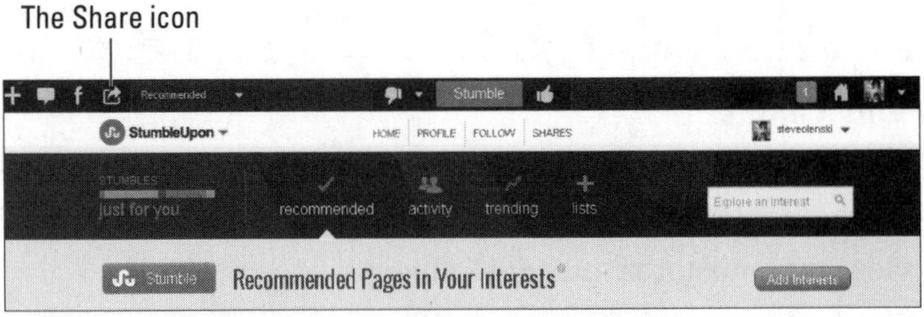

The Share icon

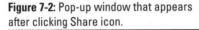

Figure 7-1: The Share icon at the top of the screen.

2. **A pop-up window appears. (See Figure 7-2.)**

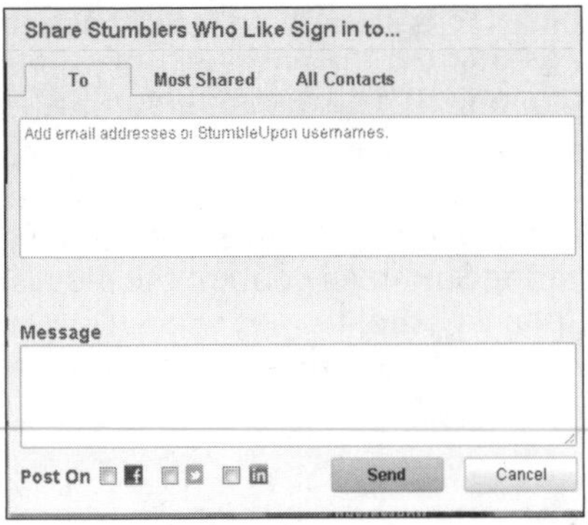

Figure 7-2: Pop-up window that appears
after clicking Share icon.

3. **In the window that appears you have the option to:**
   - Share the content via e-mail or by their StumbleUpon
     account name.
   - Share this content with those Stumblers you have
     shared the most content with in the past (Most Shared).
   - Choose from all your StumbleUpon contacts (All
     Contacts.)

- Include a message via the Message Box at the bottom.

- And share this content via one of three social media networks: Facebook, Twitter, or LinkedIn. See the next section on sharing via social media.

4. **Make a choice and let the sharing begin.**

Sharing Across Social Media Networks

It's a socially connected world we live in, right? So, of course you'll want to share your Stumble with all your friends across the various social media networks — even those friends who haven't yet joined the StumbleUpon juggernaut.

It's just as easy to share with all your social media friends, too. And StumbleUpon doesn't discriminate when it comes to which social media network you can use: From within StumbleUpon's borders, you can share your Stumble via Facebook, Twitter, or LinkedIn. To share a Stumble via Facebook, do the following:

1. **Click either the Facebook icon (see Figure 7-3) or the Share icon (refer to Figure 7-1) at the top left of the screen or on the StumbleBar.**

   If you click the Facebook icon, you'll see a window open. The URL or website address will be present in this window, along with the title or headline of the particular page you're sharing. (See Figure 7-3.)

Post on Facebook

Share 25 Spectacular Movies You (Probably)...
http://www.highexistence.com/25-spectacular-movies-you-pr...

Send   Cancel

Figure 7-3: Facebook share window.

2. **(Optional) If desired, add a message to accompany your timeline posting.**

3. **Click Send.**

   Your Share (along with any optional message) wends its way to your Facebook Timeline.

If you click the Share icon (either at the top of the screen or on the StumbleBar), a more generic window opens. (Refer to Figure 7-2.) From there, click the Facebook icon at the lower left to access the Facebook share window.

To share a stumble via Twitter or LinkedIn, click the Share icon at the top of the screen or StumbleBar, click either the Twitter or LinkedIn icon (or both) as shown in Figure 7-2, add a message (if desired) in the window that appears, and then click Send.

Keep your sharing across social media networks at a manageable level; you don't want to overload your friends and family with too much information.

Connecting or disconnecting social networks accounts

There may come a time when you want to "link" or "unlink" one or more of your social media accounts from your StumbleUpon account. For example, you may have just joined LinkedIn and now want to connect it to your StumbleUpon Account.

Or you may decide you want to disconnect your Twitter account from your StumbleUpon account because you want to keep them separate.

Adding and/or removing a link from your StumbleUpon account to a social media account is quite simple, requiring only a few easy steps:

1. **Log on to your StumbleUpon account at StumbleUpon.com.**

2. **Click the down-arrow (either in the upper-right corner of the screen, beside your profile picture on the StumbleBar, or alongside your Profile picture on StumbleUpon.com, shown in Figure 7-4) and then choose Settings from the drop-down menu that appears.**

Figure 7-4: The down-arrow button that appears adjacent to your picture and name.

3. **On the new screen that appears, click the Connected Accounts link.**

   Yet another new window appears. (See Figure 7-5.)

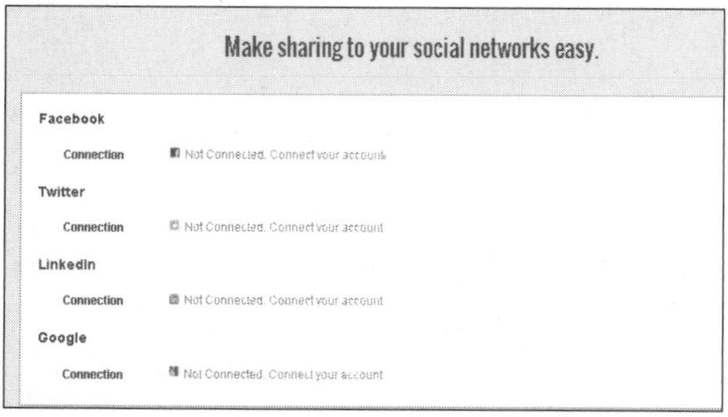

Make sharing to your social networks easy.

Facebook
   Connection   Not Connected. Connect your account

Twitter
   Connection   Not Connected. Connect your account

LinkedIn
   Connection   Not Connected. Connect your account

Google
   Connection   Not Connected. Connect your account

Figure 7-5: Options that appear after clicking Connected Accounts.

4. **To connect a social media account, simply click the Connect Your Account link.**

5. **For each social media network you want to connect to your StumbleUpon account, you'll be prompted to login to each network separately. (See Figure 7-6.)**

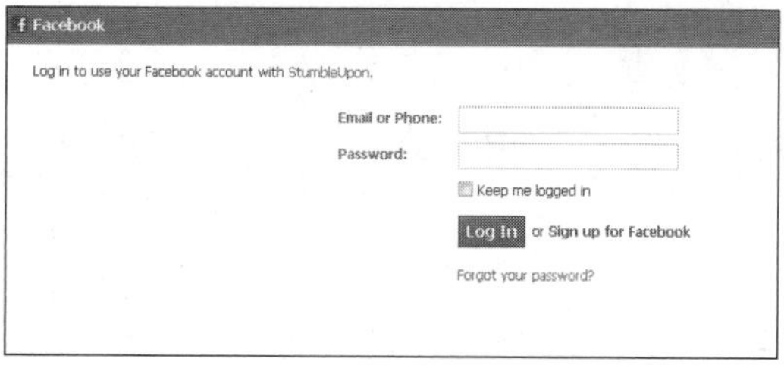

f Facebook

Log in to use your Facebook account with StumbleUpon.

Email or Phone:

Password:

Keep me logged in

Log In   or Sign up for Facebook

Forgot your password?

Figure 7-6: Facebook login screen to connect to StumbleUpon.

6. **To unlink your StumbleUpon account from one of your social media accounts, just click its associated Unlink link.**

Sharing or disabling sharing activity to Facebook automatically

If you were to take a look at the Connected Accounts tab on your Profile page, you'd see an option under Facebook that reads, "Add my activities to Facebook Timeline." (See Figure 7-7.)

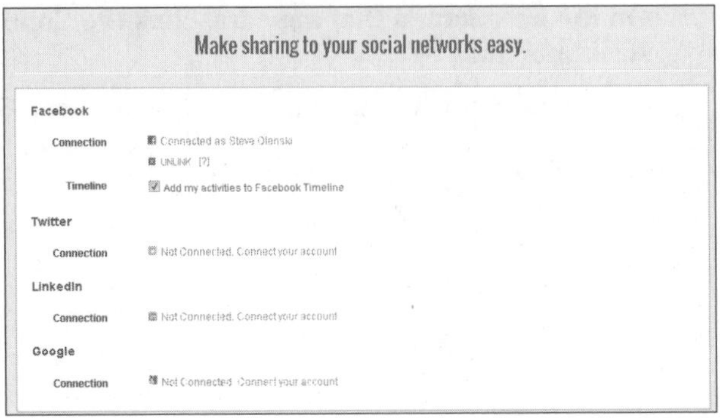

Make sharing to your social networks easy.

Facebook

Connection ☐ Connected as Steve Olenski
☐ UNLINK [?]

Timeline ☑ Add my activities to Facebook Timeline

Twitter

Connection ☐ Not Connected. Connect your account

LinkedIn

Connection ☐ Not Connected. Connect your account

Google

Connection ☐ Not Connected. Connect your account

Figure 7-7: Check box to enable or disable automatic sharing of your Stumbles to your Facebook Timeline.

By keeping the check box selected, you'll automatically be sharing all your StumbleUpon Likes and Additions directly to your Facebook Timeline. To stop this automatic sharing of your Likes and Shares, simply deselect the check box. (You may see a popup window appear with the message "setting saved"; just click OK to continue.)

Blocking Shares from Other Stumblers

Not all sharing is good sharing. At some time, you may get a Share from a Stumbler that you neither like nor want. Regardless of the reason behind your dislike or total lack of interest, you *can* take steps to ensure that you never receive Shares from this particular Stumbler again.

To see how this works, imagine that you've just opened some shared content sent to you by a Stumbler and your immediate response is "Ugh." After you get over that "Ugh" feeling, look for a panel below the StumbleBar. (See Figure 7-8.) It should contain the following information:

✔ The Stumbler who sent you the Share

✔ Any personal message if one was included

✔ A Stop Shares from This User link on the far right

socialrobinson said: Thought you find this useful...   Stop shares from this user   **View & Reply**

Figure 7-8: The panel that appears upon opening shared content from another Stumbler.

If you were to click this Stop Shares from This User link, you'd never receive a shared piece of content from this Stumbler again. (And, given this Stumbler's track record, you're probably not missing much.)

Seeing All Received and Sent Shares

You have tons of options when it comes to seeing all the Shares you have received — plus all those you have shared with others.

Start out by checking your StumbleUpon Home page, where you can get an overview of all Shares you've either received or sent.

To see how this works, first log in to your StumbleUpon account and then look for the Shares tab on your StumbleUpon Home page. Click the Shares tab to be transported to the Your Shares page, which will look something like what is shown in Figure 7-9.

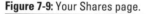

Figure 7-9: Your Shares page.

Note that the Your Shares page offers you three options to choose from:

- ✓ **All:** Choose this option if you want to view both received *and* sent Shares together.

- ✓ **Received:** Choose this option if you only want to view Shares that other Stumblers have sent you.

- ✓ **Sent:** Choose this option to see only those Shares you sent to other Stumblers.

Another way to see your received and sent Shares is by clicking the little number at the upper right of the StumbleBar. (See Figure 7-10.)

Your number of shares

Figure 7-10: The number at the upper right of the screen.

The number tells you just how many unread Shares, Updates, or Messages that are waiting for you to read, respond, and comment on.

When you click this number, you see a screen similar to what you see in Figure 7-11. The links shown here are as follows:

✔ **The number of new Shares you have waiting for you from other Stumblers.** When you click this number, you're taken to the same page as previously mentioned, where you can view all your Shares or view either received or sent Shares separately.

✔ **The number of new Messages you have waiting to be read.**

✔ **The number of new Updates you have waiting to be read.**

Figure 7-11: How many Shares, Updates, or Messages that are waiting for you to read, respond, or comment on.

The number appears on-screen until you have read all your Messages and Updates.

Clearing All Unseen Shares

Perhaps you're very popular and you have not only lots of people following you on StumbleUpon but also lots of people you follow, as well. Also, maybe all your friends share a lot of content with you — so much so that you find that you can't keep up with it all.

Now you're wondering if you have a way to clear all those Shares that you have not had time to see yet. In short, no. Unfortunately, you don't have a quick way to wipe the slate clean in terms of clearing all your unseen Shares at once.

You *can* clear your unseen Shares — but it turns out you have to do it one Share at a time. To get the spring-cleaning started, go to your Shares tab. Then next to every Share that you want to mark as seen, simply click the Mark as Read flag, which can be found in the lower-right corner of every Share. (See Figure 7-12.)

The Mark as Read flag

Figure 7-12: The flag to clear unseen Shares.

Chapter 8

Navigating the Recommended, Activity, Trending, and Lists Sections

*S*tumbleUpon is a fantastic tool for discovering new content that is tailored to your specific Interests. We wouldn't have written this book if we didn't think this were the case! But in all seriousness, StumbleUpon is also able to serve you the content you want in many different ways. Your content view choices here range from recommendations to Stumbler activity to trends to lists.

From your point of view, this should make sense, as you want the most personalized experience possible as an end user. From a content publisher's point of view, it is a win-win situation because it establishes multiple ways for the publisher's work to show up on StumbleUpon. As you become familiar with these features, you'll grow to love them.

In this chapter, we show you the ins and outs of recommendations, activities, trends, and lists, and show you how these particular features improve and personalize your experience on StumbleUpon.

Understanding the Recommended Section

Your starting point, as always, is the StumbleUpon.com Home page. The first thing that you see when you reach the Home page of Stumbleupon.com is the Recommended Pages in Your Interests section. When you first sign up for StumbleUpon, you pick and choose which Interest categories you prefer. (Refer to Chapter 2 to find how to set up and edit Interests — if you haven't done so already). If you forget what your interests are, it is easy to get a little reminder by clicking the Profile link at the top center of any page on StumbleUpon. Then click the Interests link, which brings you to a page where all the Interests you're currently following are displayed, as shown in Figure 8-1.

Now go back to the Home page to view your Recommended Pages in Your Interests section. (*Note:* To get back to the Home page, all you have to do is click the StumbleUpon Icon in the upper-left side of every page on the site.) We happen to like business-related content, so you'll see mostly business-related categories in our section, as shown in Figure 8-2.

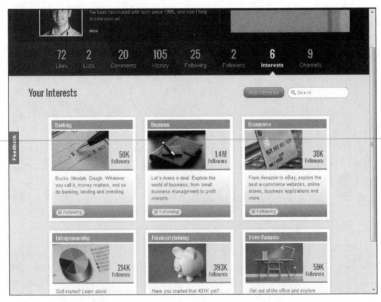

Figure 8-1: Click the Interests link on your Profile page to view all Interests you are currently following.

You now have two options on how to proceed:

✔ Click the orange Stumble button next to the Recommended Pages in Your Interests section at the upper-left corner of the page. (Refer to Figure 8-2.) Clicking the Stumble button takes you directly to a web page that is in your Interests.

Figure 8-2: The Recommended Pages in Your Interests section.

✔ Click one of the Interest icons displayed in the Recommended Pages in Your Interests section. After you click the icon, you are taken directly to the web page that had originally been added to StumbleUpon. We like this option, because it reduces the time it takes to discover worthy content to share with other Stumblers. As shown in Figure 8-3, you still get a chance to see what you're getting into by viewing the title and seeing the number of likes that content has received.

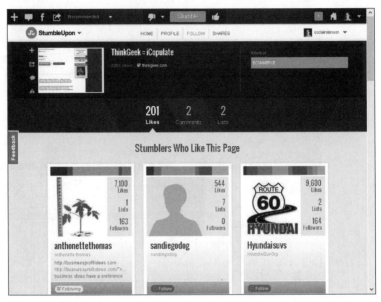

Figure 8-3: Click the See Activity link to see how Stumblers you follow are interacting with StumbleUpon content.

Using the Activity Section

If you're the type of person who wants the absolutely latest scoop on people and themes you care about, hop on over to the Activity section of the Home page. To do that, just click the Activity link near the top of the Home page on StumbleUpon.com.

In Figure 8-4, you can see that the Activity page is split into several sections. The first section you see covers the latest activity from other people you follow, or in StumbleUpon vocabulary, other Stumblers. These are the people that you follow directly on StumbleUpon, and you see all their latest activity, from creating lists to following new Stumblers to liking content.

Now, focus your attention on the various sections labeled as categories — Clothing, for example, or Advertising, or Cars. The type of content that shows up here is based on the Stumblers you follow, the StumbleUpon Experts within interests and lists you follow.

Figure 8-4: Check out the activity from Stumblers you follow directly.

For the Stumblers you follow directly, you see their respective profile picture at the bottom of the section. Click the See Activity link next to their profile picture to see how the person interacted with that particular piece of content. Most of the time, you see that the Stumbler you follow "liked" a piece of content, but you're also likely to discover that the Stumbler has commented on the content as well. (Figure 8-5 gives you an idea of what you can expect to see after clicking the See Activity link.)

As you browse the Activity section of the Home page and run into sections that display content that so-called StumbleUpon Experts have interacted with, you may find yourself asking the following questions:

✔ How do these StumbleUpon Experts show up in my Activity stream?

✔ Can we, too, become StumbleUpon Experts one day?

StumbleUpon Experts are the power users in their categories. Anytime they add new pages or interact with content, they create buzz within their category. StumbleUpon automatically qualifies StumbleUpon Experts through its own proprietary process.

Figure 8-5: Click the See Activity link to see how Stumblers you follow are interacting with StumbleUpon content.

The best advice to give for becoming a StumbleUpon Expert is to stick to a single category, follow other Stumblers, and create a relationship with them by liking and commenting on their content. Second, make sure that you are sharing truly valuable content that educates, entertains, or inspires. Becoming a StumbleUpon Expert won't happen overnight, but if you are consistent with your efforts, you too may one day be proclaimed a StumbleUpon Expert.

Uncovering Trends

Until this point in your StumbleUpon experience, you've only been seeing content that falls into the Interests you specify when signing up. *Trends* uncover the most popular content on StumbleUpon — content that may or may not overlap with your specified Interests. Timeliness and sharing activity are two factors that StumbleUpon considers when placing content into the Trends category. To view Trends, click the Trends link toward the top of the Home page on www.stumbleupon.com.

As an example, we only specify business interests in my profile, but as you can see in Figure 8-6, a lot more is going on in this world of ours than just business interests.

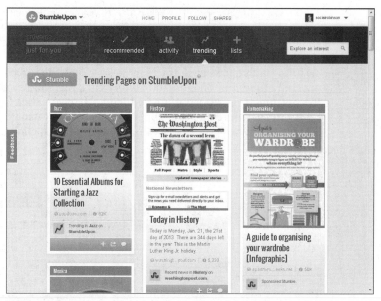

Figure 8-6: Trends show you the most timely and engaging content on StumbleUpon.

Monitoring, Following, and Sharing Lists

In the StumbleUpon world, lists are user-generated collections of content on one or more topics. All lists are kept on the StumbleUpon Home page and are a fantastic way to discover new content and to follow new Stumblers within the community. To help users navigate the different types of lists, they are organized into the following categories:

- ✔ Featured
- ✔ Recently Updated
- ✔ Most Popular

Featured lists are curated by StumbleUpon and are based on a variety of topics that might fall outside of Interests you specified during the sign-up process.

Recently Updated lists are self-explanatory. As Stumblers update their lists, StumbleUpon will update this section.

Those lists displayed in the Most Popular section have the most followers compared to other lists. These lists often have thousands of followers.

To follow a list, first click the Lists link toward the top of the Home page on stumbleupon.com and simply click the Follow button at the bottom of the appropriate List icon. After you click Follow, the button turns white and the label changes to "Following." (Figure 8-7 shows you what the button looks like after you click the Follow button.)

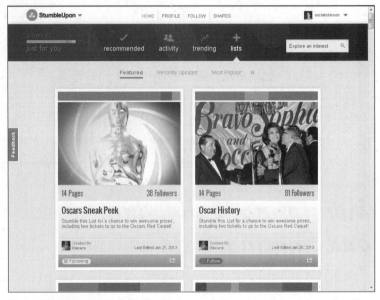

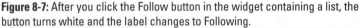

Figure 8-7: After you click the Follow button in the widget containing a list, the button turns white and the label changes to Following.

To share a list, click the Share icon in the lower right of a List icon. (The best way to describe the icon is a box with an arrow going through it.) After you click on the icon, you're presented with the option to share it directly with Stumblers you follow and who follow you back, or you can send the list to e-mail contacts. Finally, you can share the list on Facebook, Twitter, and LinkedIn. In Figure 8-8, you see what the e-mail share box looks like.

Figure 8-8: Share lists with your e-mail contacts and post to Facebook, Twitter, and LinkedIn.

As you browse through StumbleUpon, these tools and features will help you discover the best content and most engaged users. Now your job is to use them to your advantage!

Chapter 9

Using the Paid Discovery Advertising System

*S*tumbleUpon is a great platform for driving free traffic back to your website over time, but what if you need to gain traction quickly? If you have the time to build your network on StumbleUpon and share content every day, by all means forge ahead.

If you don't have the time (which most people don't nowadays), you have three options. And you can use all three if you wish:

- ✔ Hire someone to do all the organic outreach for you. (Can be pricey.)

- ✔ Use an intern. (You still have to train him or her, which equals time spent training the person when you could be doing something else.)

- ✔ Use Paid Discovery. (Still not free, but potentially a better value than the Hiring Someone option.)

The last item in the list is the quickest way to catapult your content into the spotlight, especially if you're not well known or need to raise awareness and drive revenue.

Paid Discovery is StumbleUpon's advertising service and is the primary method it has of making money for the site. Essentially, you pay to promote your content to a specific demographic and within a select few Interest categories. An advantage of using Paid

Discovery is that you only pay for every click that leads to your website, nothing else. Essentially it's pay for performance. The performance comes in the form of clicks.

Understanding Paid Discovery versus Paid Search

Before we get into the major differences, let's go over the definitions of Paid Search and Paid Discovery.

What's a Paid Search?

In simple terms, *Paid Search* is paying for ad placements in search engines based on keywords used by searchers. It is common for advertisers to only pay a fee when their advertisements are clicked. The price of the clicks are determined by a number of factors including (but not limited to) what competitors are willing to pay for each keyword, keyword relevance to the ad, and the experience after the click, which is called the landing page. Ads are placed at the top or right side of the results page after you search for a keyword. In Figure 9-1, you see what a Paid Search advertisement looks like on Google.com.

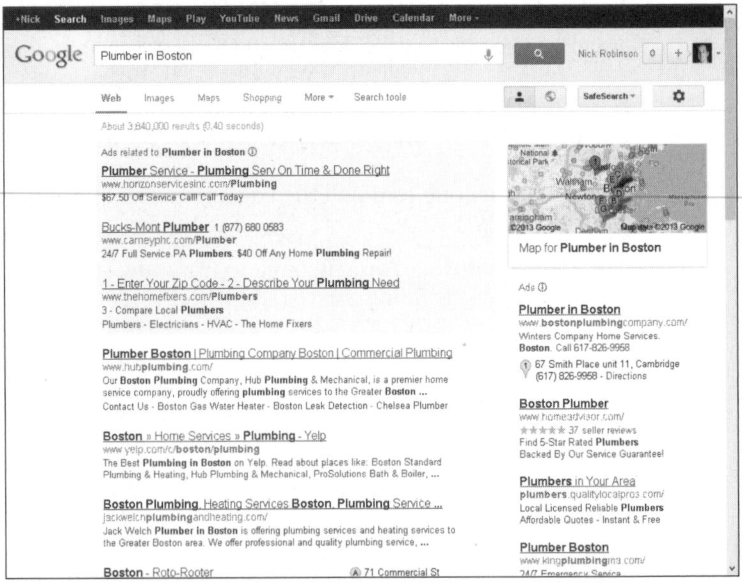

Figure 9-1: This is what a Paid Search ad looks like if you search for the keyword, "Plumber in Boston".

What's a Paid Discovery?

Paid Discovery is the advertising system used by StumbleUpon, where advertisers pay for their web pages to be placed in the home page stream on StumbleUpon.com or the StumbleUpon mobile application. Paid Discovery placements appear to be normal pieces of content. To identify Paid Discovery content, you see a green icon or "Sponsored" label in the StumbleUpon toolbar at the top of the webpage or at the bottom of each content widget in the different content streams through StumbleUpon. In Figure 9-2, you see what a Paid Discovery placement looks like if you randomly Stumble the content or if you click on the content in a feed within StumbleUpon.

Look for "Sponsored"

Figure 9-2: This is what a Paid Discovery ad placement looks like in the StumbleUpon toolbar at the top of the webpage.

The business models for Paid Discovery and Paid Search are quite similar in that they derive revenue from clicks; the revenue is based on pay per click. *Pay per click* means that, as an advertiser, you only pay a fee when someone clicks on an ad placement within the website or application.

While many similarities exist, you find some key differences in the way that an advertiser uses each method and how much he actually pays. We take a closer look at each channel to see those differences.

Targeting your audience

Paid Discovery is designed to target people who are looking to "discover" new places, people, or things. With this notion of people casually browsing for new things, paying to promote your content on StumbleUpon generates awareness, leads, and sales. How long it takes to generate actual revenue depends on a multitude of factors, but the leading indicator for your sales cycle will be the complexity of a purchase decision and what your company does to demonstrate value.

Paid Search, on the other hand, is designed for many purposes, but mainly it is used for direct marketing for generating leads and driving revenue. The majority of search users are looking for specific information or products. They aren't using a search engine to discover random things. These people are a little farther in their purchasing decision than a Paid Discovery target.

Paying the (StumbleUpon) piper

When implementing a Paid Discovery campaign, you pay a flat fee per unique visitor. The fee you pay depends on what kind of exposure you want to receive. In Table 9-1, you see a breakdown of the packages offered by StumbleUpon.

Table 9-1   Paid Discovery Package Comparison

Standard	Premium	Custom
Priority serving in content streams	Guaranteed top serving priority	Build a custom program
Target by interest, location, demographics	Standard targeting options	Outside the box
Advanced targeting by device (web or mobile)	Standard campaign targeting options	RFP (Request for Proposal)
Advanced reporting and Integration with Google Analytics	Advanced reporting and Integration with Google Analytics	Advanced reporting and Integration with Google Analytics

Paid Search campaigns are different in that you bid for keywords based on an auction format. The price you pay for each keyword and in what position your ads show up are based on a number of factors, including

> ✔ How many competitors are bidding for each keyword
>
> ✔ What your competitors are actually bidding for each keyword
>
> ✔ The relevancy of your ad to the keyword
>
> ✔ The relevancy of your website to the keyword and ad

If you search for "Plumber in Boston", the Paid Search ad would show up at the top or right of the search results page. See Figure 9-2 for examples of what the ads look like.

Paid Discovery versus Banner Ads

Before we go into the differences between Paid Discovery and banner ads, here is a little definition of what banner ads are.

Banner ads are advertisements placed within a web page that are designed to attract the attention of the reader, listener, or video watcher. They are often designed to increase awareness or to encourage clicks to an offer or promotion.

Maybe you're still on the fence about using Paid Discovery or banner ads. Before you dive into the how-to's of a Paid Discovery campaign, it is important to understand the difference, as seen in Table 9-2.

Table 9-2	Paid Discovery versus Banner Ads	
Campaign Type	*Exposure*	*User Engagement*
Paid Discovery	Targeted	Clicks and sharing are the foundation
Banner ads	Widespread	Limited/passive. Website visitors usually don't click on these, and you can't share a banner ad easily.

Now that you are familiar with the differences between Paid Discovery and banner ads, it's time to do some strategizing. You need to ask yourself what your business goals are. If it is widespread impression-based exposure with a touch of direct marketing, banner ads will fulfill your needs. If your goal is impression and engagement-based exposure, Paid Discovery could be your choice.

Of course, banner ads certainly produce engagement, which is in the form of clicks to your website. But it's easy to leave a web page after one click, so don't think it's going to be an easy sale without considering other factors (factors outside the scope of this book, to be honest.) With Paid Discovery, you have multiple ways of amplifying the reach of your content through sharing, likes, comments, and clicks. If you're producing quality content, you'll eventually see leads and revenue.

The goal here isn't to convince you that one option is better than the other. Your business is different than every other business out there, and it would be foolish to discourage you from implementing banner ads just because this book is about StumbleUpon. The goal here is to educate you on what channels are available to you on the StumbleUpon platform. We will take you through the platform in a couple of sections. Make sense? Good; we'll carry on, then.

Using Social Media Elements

The beauty of Paid Discovery is that your promoted content has social elements as a foundation. Not only are you reaching a defined audience, but your content's reach is also amplified through social sharing, which you don't have to pay for. You only pay for unique visitors to your website or blog.

For example, if you want to promote a video using Paid Discovery that is hosted on your site and many different visitors like or share the content, that is free exposure that you wouldn't have gotten if you didn't use Paid Discovery on StumbleUpon.

The following sections describe some of the ways that Stumblers can click, share, like, your content through social media elements.

Likes

If your content resonates with your audience, a quick way for them to give their feedback is to click the Like button on their StumbleUpon toolbar. In the main page of StumbleUpon, you see how many likes a piece of content has by looking at the number toward the bottom of each widget. Content that has a large of likes indicates that is regarded as quality by the StumbleUpon community, precisely why you want your content to be liked. Figure 9-3 shows you what this looks like.

Figure 9-3: Stumblers who visit your site click the Like button to give them approval.

Add to List

Stumblers use lists for two main purposes, including

- ✔ Content curation to provide value for their followers
- ✔ Collecting a vault of content for future reference

Anytime someone adds your content to a list, this counts as engagement, which gives your content more reach over time. When you promote a piece of content using Paid Discovery, you increase the chance of users adding that content to their lists (which is free by the way; you only pay for the original click!)

Sharing

You have a multitude of ways to share using the StumbleUpon toolbar. Anytime a Stumbler performs one of these actions, it gives your content greater reach. For free! Here are some of the ways StumbleUpon users can share your content.

- ✔ Facebook
- ✔ Twitter

✔ Direct Share with another Stumbler

✔ E-mail

So when thinking about using Paid Discovery, you can calculate the return by spreading the budget over all the organic sharing that results from promoting your content. It always drives down the initial cost.

Here is a simple formula that we use:

(Total Budget/Total Clicks) – [Total Shares * (Total Budget/ Total Clicks)] = Total Budget Reduction from Free Shares

Let's plug in some numbers. Your budget was $100 and you received 400 clicks and 50 shares.

($100/400) – [50 * ($100/400)] = -12.25

You shaved off $12.25 of your budget due to your content having received 50 free shares. Imagine if you had 400 shares. *Hint:* You'd be paying a total of $0.25 for Paid Discovery! Now you'll still actually be paying the money, but this is a good formula to calculate the value of free sharing as a result of promoting your content with Paid Discovery.

Launching a Paid Discovery Campaign

Now it's time to set up and launch your Paid Discovery campaign.

The first thing you do is type **www.stumbleupon.com/pd** into the web address bar at the top of your browser. Press Enter. The next page displays an intro to Paid Discovery. Click the blue Get Started button. If you don't have an account, you need to sign up.

To sign up for a Paid Discovery account, first click the Create Account link, then you need to enter your e-mail address and password (enter the password twice) in the fields provided; then accept the terms and conditions by selecting the check box. After you click the Submit button, StumbleUpon sends an activation e-mail to the address you provided during the sign-up process. Open the e-mail and click the activation link.

Upon activating the link, you are taken to the Create a New Paid Discovery Campaign page, as seen in Figure 9-4. Here you enter the web address that you want to promote, then enter how much traffic you want to drive to your website on a daily basis. This will determine how much you pay per day. After you've entered the web address and set the daily budget and traffic numbers, click the blue Save and Review button.

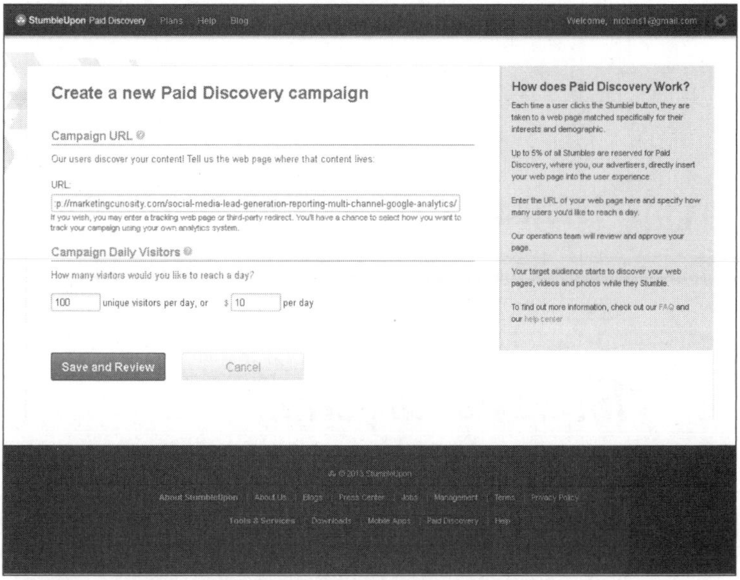

Figure 9-4: Setting up your Paid Discovery campaign.

On the new page that appears — see Figure 9-5 — you'll be asked to come up with a name for your Paid Discovery campaign. The idea here is to settle on a name that best describes the campaign intention. For example, you could name your campaign Blog Content Promotion 1, if you're trying to get your blog content in front of more people.

It's always best to number your campaigns sequentially so that you can distinguish among the different campaigns that you run.

Figure 9-5: The default screen for setting up your campaign name, your demographic and interests targeting, your budget, and your campaign schedule.

Interests targeting

When you're trying to reach a specific audience, you want to "target" the types of people you "believe" will interact with your advertising. This is really important in any type of marketing, since you don't want the wrong types of people clicking on your content and then abandoning your website right away.

For targeting criteria, one choice you have with StumbleUpon involves Interests Bundles, which are broad interest groups that match the *psychograhics* — the combination of user behaviors that make up a common profile — for each group that you want to reach. Essentially, StumbleUpon has enough information about these broad groups of users to know that they will interact with certain types of content. These users are more likely to click and share your Paid Discovery content.

Your other choice is Precise Targeting, where you choose to target interests manually.

We recommend sticking with the Interest Bundles targeting, as StumbleUpon's advertising system is smart enough to make changes on the fly, rather than you going into the system every day. We would reserve the manual process for more advanced users.

To choose Interest Bundles, first click to select its radio button, as seen in Figure 9-6, then click to select one of the many options you havefor targeting. For example, if you're promoting extreme sports content, you'd want to target adrenaline junkies. To choose multiple Interest Bundles, press the Ctrl key and click another Interest Bundle.

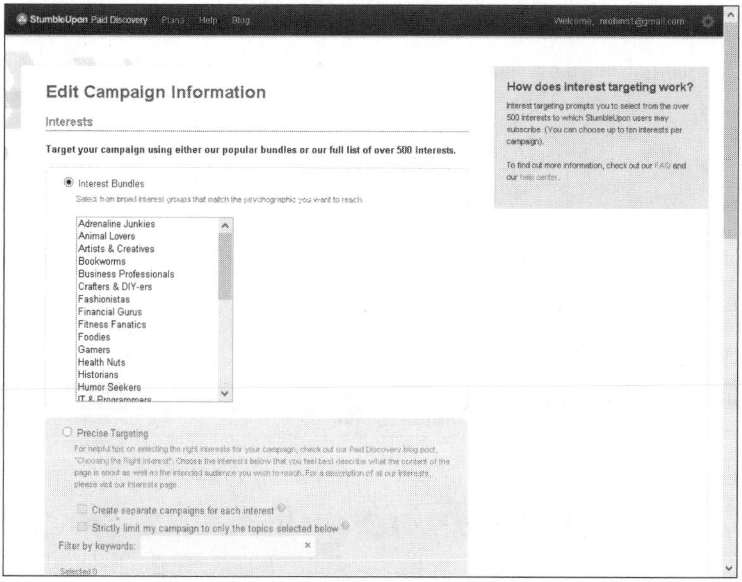

Figure 9-6: Selecting among the various Interest Bundle targeting options.

To choose your interest targets manually, click to select the Precise Targeting. Radio button. (Refer to Figure 9-6.) with this option, you have the opportunity to drill down into specific interests that your target audience will be most interested in. If you want to separate each precise interest into its own campaign, you do so by selecting the Create Separate Campaigns for Each Interest check box. This allows you to manually optimize each interest based on its performance. If you want to restrict targeting specifically to the interests chosen, select the Strictly Limit My Campaign to Only the Topics Selected Below check box. This controls your daily spend and targeting. If you don't select this check box, StumbleUpon will serve your content to related and adjacent topics. In Figure 9-7, you can see how you can start out with a broader category and then drill down into specific topics.

When you're done editing your interest targeting, click the blue Save and Review button. (It's cut off in Figure 9-7, but you'll see it on your screen.)

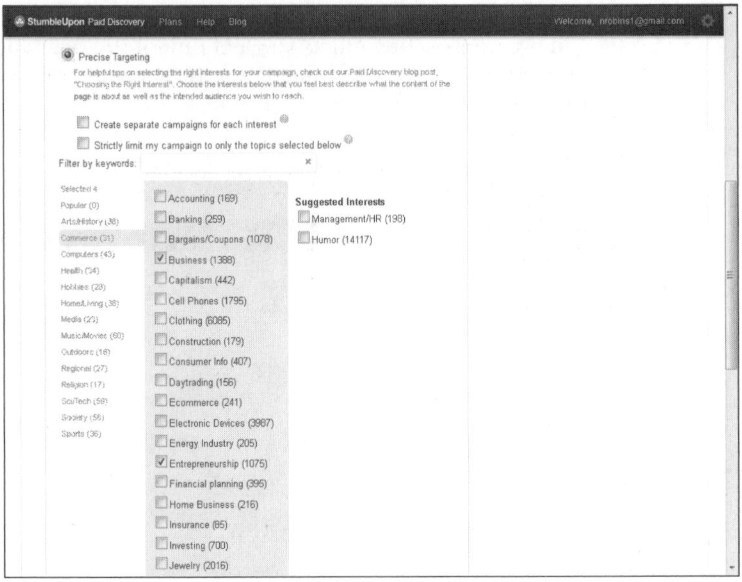

Figure 9-7: Precise targeting allows you to drill down into specific interests that your audience will interact with.

Demographic and device targeting

The next section of the Paid Discovery campaign setup process involves choosing your demographic and device targeting. By default, everything is set to *Auto*, meaning that the target demographics will be chosen by StumbleUpon based on who they think will interact with your adds. Consequently, you have less control over who you're reaching and what devices — desktop computer internet browsers, mobile phones, or mobile tablets — your Paid Discovery appears on. We suggest going in manually and choosing demographics and devices. To manually choose your demographics and devices, click Edit to the right of the Demographics & Device heading. (Refer to Figure 9-5.) On the next page, you're greeted with the two main options: Auto or Manual.

To manually choose your demographic and device targeting, click the Manual radio button, as seen in Figure 9-8. After you click the radio button, the background color will change from gray to white, which means that you'll now be able to change the various settings.

For age targeting, you see a scale with blue-and-white squares on both ends of the scale. To narrow the age range, click each box and drag until the age range changes to your desired targeting.

For example, if you have a blog article about living with arthritis, you'd want to target people that are a little bit older. Whereas a blog post or video about Lady Gaga would probably skew to a much younger audience, say 20-somethings.

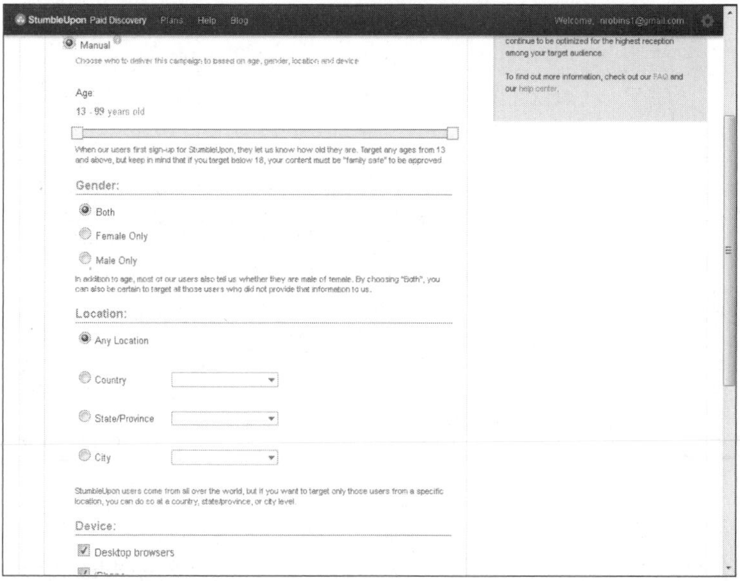

Figure 9-8: Manually choose the demographic and device targeting for your Paid Discovery campaign.

For gender targeting, you have three choices:

✔ Both

✔ Female Only

✔ Male Only

Click the radio button that makes the most sense for your business goals and strategy.

For example, if you're a women's fashion blog, you'll probably want to target only women. If you're a men's ice hockey video site, you're probably going to want to target men. Get the point?

For location targeting, you have the choice of Any Location, or you can drill down to Country, State, or City.

Finally, choose among the following devices:

- ✔ Desktop browsers
- ✔ iPhone
- ✔ Android
- ✔ iPad
- ✔ Android Tablet

Select each check box for the device that makes sense for your business goals and strategy. If you're happy with your demographic and device targeting choices, click the blue Save and Review button. (Again, this is cut off in Figure 9-8, but you're sure to see it on your screen.)

With all this being said, we suggest that you stick with the Auto format if you're a beginner. Then, as you become more familiar with Paid Discovery, you can choose your own interests and demographics.

Serving priority

In this stage of the Paid Discovery campaign setup process, you choose the priority given to your content based on StumbleUpon's ad inventory. You'll pay more to have your content prioritized in the Paid Discovery ad system. Essentially, paying a bit more means your ads take precedence over content in lower price levels. You have three serving priority options:

- ✔ **Highest:** Serves first ($0.25 per visitor)
- ✔ **Normal:** Available after highest priority ($0.10 per visitor)
- ✔ **Lowest:** Remaining availability given ($0.05 per visitor)

By default, the serving priority is set to Normal. To change the priority, click Edit to the right of the Serving Priority heading. (Refer to Figure 9-5.) On the new page that appears, as seen in Figure 9-9, you're presented with the three priority options with radio buttons to the left. Click the priority option that best fits your budget.

After you are happy with your serving priority settings, click the blue Save and Review button.

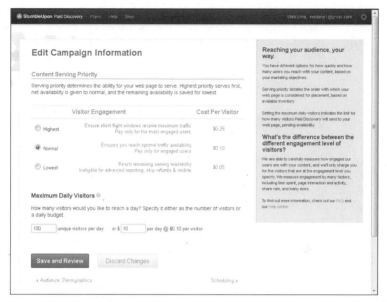

Figure 9-9: Choose the serving priority that best fits your budget and timeline.

Scheduling

By default, your Paid Discovery campaign starts automatically upon approval and has no end date. Based on your business goals and how Paid Discovery weaves into your promotional schedule, you have three ways for your campaign to end:

✓ When your specified budget runs out

✓ When you pause your campaign

✓ When you specify an end date (option to schedule a start date too)

To specify a start and end date for your Paid Discovery campaign, click Edit to the right of the Start heading. (Refer Figure 9-3.) On the new page that appears, you have two options for scheduling, as shown in Figure 9-10. The first option is Auto, which is where your campaign runs as long as you have funds on account or up until that time when you decide to pause the campaign yourself. The second option is Manual, where you specify a start and end date. If you want your campaign to start automatically upon approval, leave the Start Date option as is. To specify a different start date, click the field below the Start Date heading, and a calendar box appears. Click the day of the month you'd like to start your campaign. To specify an end date, click the field below the End Date heading, and a calendar box appears. Click the day of the month you'd like to end your campaign.

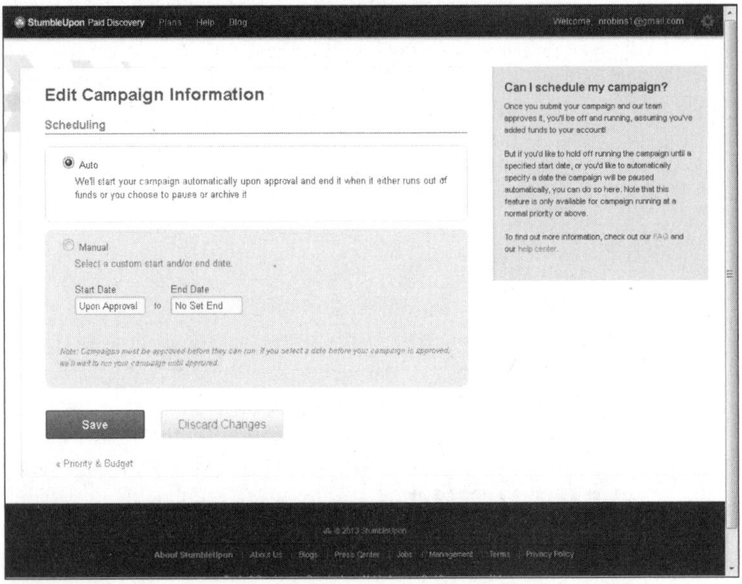

Figure 9-10: Your options for scheduling your Paid Discovery campaign.

When you're happy with your campaign schedule settings, click the blue Save button. You're now finished setting up your Paid Discovery campaign! Click the blue Create Campaign button. Next, you need to add funds to your campaign. You have the option of paying by credit card or through PayPal.

Determining Whether Paid Discovery Worked

After a couple of days of running a Paid Discovery campaign, data is now ready to be analyzed. This begs the question: How do you know whether Paid Discovery is working?

Calculating exposure

For exposure, you look at total traffic generated and sharing activity. In traditional marketing, the metrics commonly used for exposure are *impressions* and *engagement.* An impression is technically every time someone *might* see your content, so impression is calculated every time the StumbleUpon feed page is loaded. Engagement is when someone actual does something, like click through to your website or share with others. Because StumbleUpon doesn't provide impression-based reporting, We'll use engagement as the primary metric here. Next, you'll want to calculate the campaign costs. The costs are as follows:

✔ Content production

✔ Marketing staff overhead

✔ Paid Discovery spending

Now take the sum of campaign costs and divide by the total engagements (traffic and sharing). This is called *cost per engagement.* Now, compare the cost per engagement of Paid Discovery to other channels in your marketing mix like Paid Search, Events, TV ads, Radio, etc. You'll get a really good bottom-line sense of the performance of your Paid Discovery campaign.

Calculating leads

For leads, you'll have to do a little setup with your web analytics service. It's fairly easy to set up in Google Analytics, which is the most common (and free) web analytics service. Here's how to do it.

First, sign up for a Google Analytics account if you don't have one already. Then type www.google.com/analytics in the web address bar at the top of your browser. After signing into Google Analytics, click the Admin link located in the upper right of the page. Click your profile name, and then click Goals on the next page.

If you've already set up a couple of goals, you see a list of them here. To add a new goal, click +Goal. Name the goal, so it's easily identified in reports. Click the Active radio button, and then click the URL Destination radio button. Figure 9-11 shows what the page looks like when filled out with the appropriate information.

If you have Thank You pages set up after someone submits his or her contact information — and we highly suggest you do this — copy and paste the last part of the web address into the Goal URL field. For example, if your Thank You page address is `http://www.marketingcuriosity.com/thanks-for-interest`, copy and paste `/thanks-for-interest` into the Goal URL field. Then choose Exact Match on the Match Type drop-down menu. *Exact Match* means that Google Analytics will only record the goal if the last part of the web address matches the Thank You page exactly.

If you know what a lead is worth to you as a business, enter the dollar amount (without the $) in the Goal Value field.

Finally, click Save, and your goal is now set up.

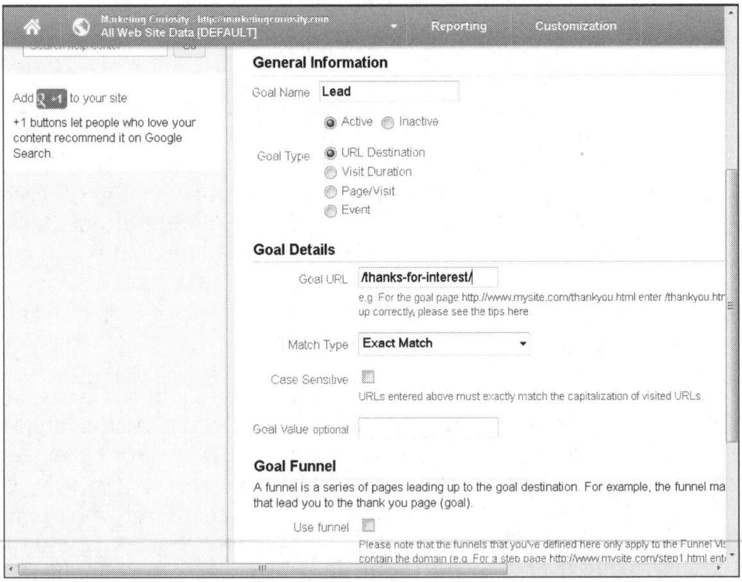

![Screenshot of Google Analytics goal setup showing General Information with Goal Name "Lead", Goal Type "URL Destination", Goal Details with Goal URL "/thanks-for-interest/", Match Type "Exact Match", and Goal Funnel sections.]

Figure 9-11: Setting up goals in Google Analytics.

Make sure to set up goals in Google Analytics before you launch a Paid Discovery campaign, or you lose valuable data for analyzing lead generation!

The calculation to use for lead generation is cost per lead. Add up all the leads generated during the Paid Discovery campaign and divide them by the sum of your campaign costs. Now compare Paid Discovery cost per lead to other channels in your marketing mix.

Revenue

To get to your revenue numbers and attribute them to a specific marketing channel, you need to have e-commerce tracking set up if you sell products or services directly on your website. Or, you need to pull your web analytics stats into your Customer Relationship Management (CRM) software program. After you start importing web analytics into your CRM software, you can attribute revenue to Paid Discovery.

Google Analytics has a really good e-commerce tracking option, and High Rise or Salesforce are good options as your CRM systems.

You need to look at total revenue and average order value. Average order value is the average amount of money someone pays you at checkout. Take these two metrics and compare them against other channels in your marketing mix.

Optimizing your campaign

After you analyze the data and determine what's working and what's not, it's time to make some tweaks to your campaign to do more of the good and less of the bad.

First, make another visit to `www.stumbleupon.com/pd` and sign in using your Paid Discovery username and password. Next, click Reports on the navigation menu on the left side of the page.

On the next page, specify the following criteria that you want to have addressed in your report, using the drop-down menus shown in Figure 9-12. They are as follows:

- ✔ Date Range
- ✔ URL (web address)
- ✔ Campaign
- ✔ Topic
- ✔ Device
- ✔ Age Range
- ✔ Gender
- ✔ Country
- ✔ State

To keep the analysis simple, set all the drop-down menus to All so that you are able to compare the various criteria against each other. Click Generate Report.

When the page reloads, you see a nice-looking chart that gives you a breakdown of traffic, engagement, and sharing metrics. (Figure 9-13 also shows a breakdown by topic.) To see a different breakdown by gender, age range, device, country, state, or date, click the drop-down menu in the upper-left portion of the chart and make a choice there.

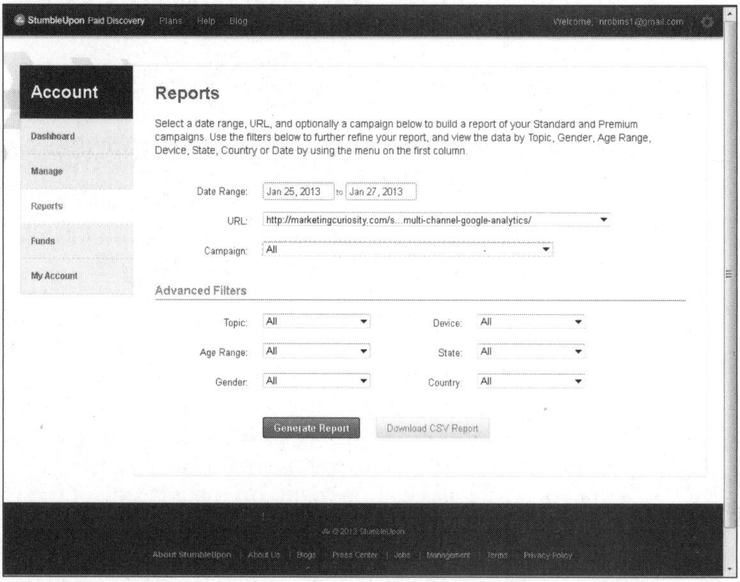

Figure 9-12: Use the Reports tool to specify date range, URL, campaign, topic, and more criteria.

In Figure 9-13, you can see that marketing and entrepreneurship are the top traffic drivers to the campaign web address. My campaign goal is to increase exposure for Marketingcuriosity.com, and the marketing topic is clearly achieving my goal. If you're the one running this campaign, just pause the campaign (it's been running for two days at this point) and relaunch a new campaign targeting only the marketing and entrepreneurship topics. The idea here is the campaign had targeted interests broader than marketing and entrepreneurship, and now you want to limit the campaign to just those topics.

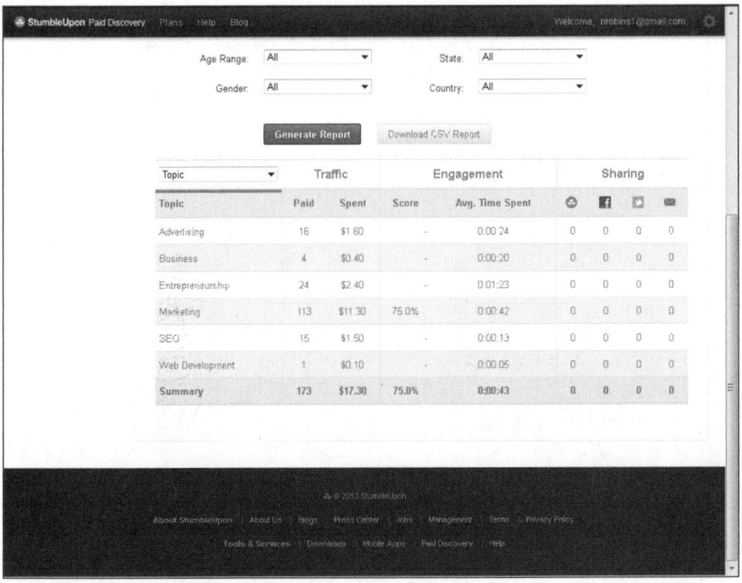

Figure 9-13: Use reports to compare different criteria.

The point of making these optimizations is to control spending by targeting the best-performing criteria within your campaign. You want to drive down the cost per engagement and cost per lead/acquisition in basically anything in marketing. The beauty of Paid Discovery is that you have the ability to optimize on the fly.

Celebrating Success — A Case Study

Adam Costa needed a big boost in exposure for his new blog called Trekity (www.trekity.com), and he turned to Paid Discovery as one of the tactical channels within his marketing strategy. His primary objective was to increase traffic, so he spent $300 on a Paid Discovery campaign. He already had a stockpile of content written, so the setup was easy.

Three thousand visitors in one day for a $300 investment! Because exposure was his business goal, his cost per engagement is $0.10. Adam also produced a Help A Reporter Out (HARO) ad, which resulted in a $2.09 cost per engagement. As you can see, Paid Discovery is the winning channel for the launch campaign.

In the end, it's worth testing Paid Discovery to give your content a boost. Now go out there and get some campaigns going!

Chapter 10

Using StumbleUpon to Generate Traffic to Your Blog or Website

. . . .

. . . .

A s a user, StumbleUpon makes your life easy by serving you content according to your interests and the people you care about. But what about the other side of the equation? That is, the content producers, in other words, those folks who take the time and make the effort to come up with the stuff you like. Without content to share, StumbleUpon wouldn't be what it is today, so first and foremost, hats off to all the great content producers out there.

Wait, you say *you're* one of those content producers? And you're curious how you can get on StumbleUpon's radar so that you can use its tools and its people to grow your website or blog?

Well, you've come to the right place, because in this chapter, you find out how to add StumbleUpon widgets and badges on your website or blog, engage in the StumbleUpon community to increase your content's reach, and produce content that Stumblers will love.

Generating Stumble-Worthy Content

First and foremost, you have to produce the right type of content to gain traction within the StumbleUpon community. In fact, this is true in all types of online marketing. Content really is king (insert cliché mention here). So how do you create content that Stumblers will love? Read on.

Know your audience

Admittedly, marketers no longer go around saying "know your audience." That's not fancy enough. The new buzzwords about knowing your audience all have to do with "persona development." Essentially, it is the process of identifying the different archetypes that will gain value from visiting your site or consuming your content. Smaller sites might have 2–3 personas, and larger sites might have 6–12 personas.

The best place to start gathering information for persona development is through asking your current audience, whether they be customers or site browsers. Surveys, phone conversations, website statistics, and asking questions on other social networks tend to be the best methods for collecting this information.

As for the kinds of questions you'll want to ask, they'll most likely revolve around your audience's demographic information and challenges, and what their typical day looks like.

On your website or blog, take a look at your website statistics. A common service is Google Analytics, and it's free. If you haven't started tracking your website statistics yet, now is the time to start! If you already have some kind of website tracking set up, take a look at your top-performing content in terms of traffic. With that info in hand, you'll probably get a good sense of what people gravitate to.

Experiment with multimedia

Now that we're in the twenty-first century, multimedia content creation is within the reach of most everyone, even those with a modest budget. Video, audio, and pictures have gained traction, so it is advisable to repurpose text-based content with video, audio, and imagery. As human beings, we are visual and auditory in nature, so it makes sense for you mix up your content formats.

Mobile phones and laptop computers tend to be equipped with cameras and microphones as standard equipment, so developing video doesn't have to be an expensive project. As long as the meat of the content you're producing is truly valuable, you have a solid foundation to build upon.

Educate, entertain, inspire

The definition of value has different meanings to each person viewing your content. Value from education often saves time and money. Value from entertainment induces an emotional reaction, whether it's laughter, crying, or something in between. Value from inspiration comes in the form of the motivation to start doing something new or persevere through something already in the works.

Content may contain one or all three of these elements. If you can fit all three into one piece of content, you're on your way to rock star status on StumbleUpon.

Adding the StumbleUpon Badge and Widget

Do you want to make it super-easy to see and share your content on StumbleUpon directly from your blog or website? If so, StumbleUpon has created a badge and widget for easy sharing. In the following sections, you find out how to implement the widget so that your content is spread through other Stumblers.

Adding the StumbleUpon badge

To add the StumbleUpon badge, enter **www.stumbleupon.com/ dt/badges** into the web address bar at the top of your browser. After you arrive at the Badge page, click the Get Started - It's Free! button.

On the next page, you get to choose the size and type of badge you want. After specifying what you want, StumbleUpon automatically generates the necessary HTML code you'll need for your website in the box to the right of the blue arrow, as shown in Figure 10-1.

Now that you have the code, you can either place the code yourself or have a web developer place the code where you want the badge to show up.

Usually, you'll find Share buttons from other social networks accompanying the StumbleUpon badge. In Figure 10-2, for example, you see what the StumbleUpon badge looks like within the group of Share buttons.

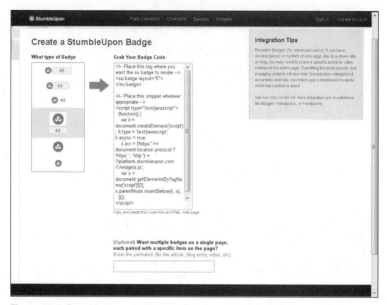

Figure 10-1: StumbleUpon automatically generates the code you need for your website or blog.

Figure 10-2: The StumbleUpon badge within a group of Share buttons.

Adding the StumbleUpon widget

After you start adding content to StumbleUpon, you have the option of adding a widget to your blog or website to showcase your most popular content. The setup process is rather easy, but make sure that you have a web developer handy if you're not familiar with website coding.

First, enter **www.stumbleupon.com/dt/widgets** into the web address bar at the top of your browser. After you arrive at the Widget page, click the Start Now - It's Free! button.

On the next page, you have two options when it comes to populating the widget on your website with content: You can either show content from individual StumbleUpon accounts or from other websites.

To show content from StumbleUpon users on your website widget, type in the username of the account you want to display. For example, if you type **socialrobinson**, all content shared from that account will display in the Preview pane, as shown in Figure 10-3.

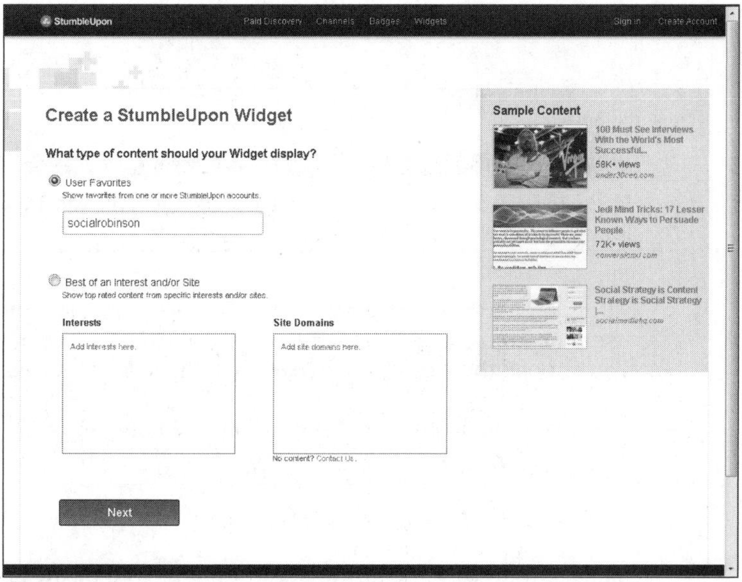

Figure 10-3: Type in the username of the account you want to display in the Preview pane of the Widget setup page.

To show content from websites, type in the domain name of the website you want to display. For example, if you type **techcrunch. com**, you will see all StumbleUpon content shared from TechCrunch. To add multiple websites, for example, type **techcrunch.com**, press Enter, and type **business2community.com**, and you will see content from both sites. What you see from both websites depends on the date of publication. All content shared from the websites you type will display in the Preview pane, as shown in Figure 10-4.

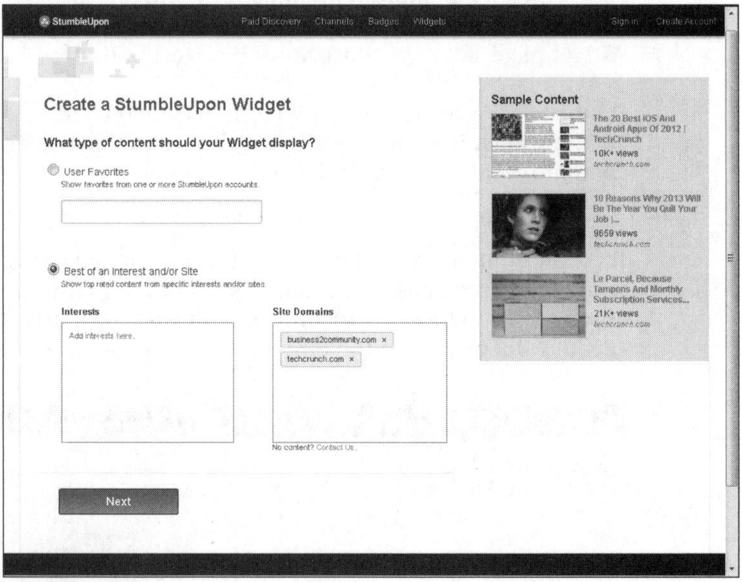

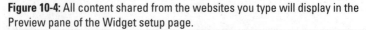

Figure 10-4: All content shared from the websites you type will display in the Preview pane of the Widget setup page.

After you choose whether to show content from StumbleUpon users or from websites, click the Next button. On the next page, you choose the size of the widget. You have three sizing options:

- ✔ Small Horizontal Rectangle (300 x 250 pixels)
- ✔ Large Horizontal Rectangle (600 x 250 pixels)
- ✔ Large Vertical Rectangle (160 x 600 pixels)

Make sure to pick the sizing option that best fits with your website design.

Next, choose a title for the widget. StumbleUpon automatically generates a title based on the website address. For example, if your website address is myblogrocks.com, the title would be "myblogrocks.com on StumbleUpon." You can edit the title as you please.

All right, you're almost finished. Note that, after making your sizing and naming decisions, StumbleUpon generates the code you need and places it in a box to the right of the sizing and title options, as shown in Figure 10-5. Copy that code and either paste it into your website code yourself or hand it off to a website developer to do it for you. That's it!

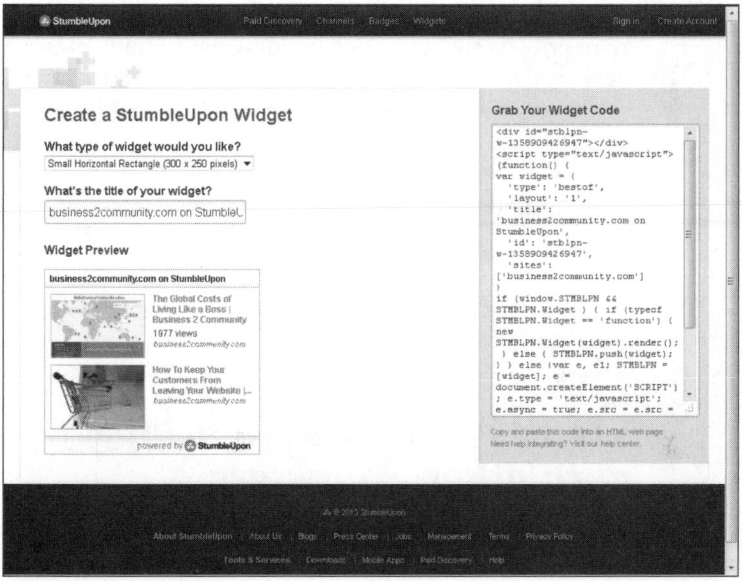

Figure 10-5: Copy and paste the widget code into your website code or hand it off to a website developer.

If you're using Wordpress, you may use several plug-ins to accomplish this same task. The previous option is more customizable if you're code-savvy.

Creating a Large StumbleUpon Network

Much like in the real world, you're not going to be very successful if you don't build a network of contacts. The same holds true if you want to dramatically increase traffic to your website or blog from StumbleUpon. The more engaged relationships you build, the more traffic and engagement you will receive as a result of your hard work.

This should be reiterated. You need to work hard to develop relationships. They take time to develop, so you shouldn't expect to be an overnight success when building your StumbleUpon network.

In the following sections, you'll find out all about

✔ Creating new relationships with other Stumblers

✔ Engaging other Stumblers

✔ Asking others to Stumble your content

Give it some time, and you'll see your website or blog traffic rise as a result of your efforts!

Creating new relationships with other Stumblers

The first thing you need to do is engage other Stumblers who are liking (and commenting on) content within your Interest categories. The best way to do this is to go to several pieces of content and find out who's doing all this engaging. Sounds hard? Not if you know the tricks of the trade.

First, go to the StumbleUpon Home page and track down the Recommended Pages in Your Interests section. Pick a headline that interests you, and at the lower right of the widget, you see a small circular icon with an *i* in the middle. (See Figure 10-6.) The number next to it represents the amount of StumbleUpon engagement on that piece of content. Click the icon and number.

The next page displays a list of all the people who have liked that particular piece of content. Go ahead and follow all those Stumblers. (If you're not sure how to do this "follow" business, check out Chapter 2.)

Next, click Comments in the upper-middle portion of the page. This section displays a list of all the Stumblers who have left a comment on the piece of content. Because these Stumblers took the time to leave a comment, you should reasonably assume that they are a more engaged segment of your Interest category. Follow these Stumblers. Then, you want to put these Stumblers on a hot list of people to forge a relationship with. A simple Excel spreadsheet will suffice.

Figure 10-6: Click the icon and number to discover which other Stumblers are engaging with the content that you're interested in.

Now, go back to the StumbleUpon Home page after you start getting notifications that Stumblers are following you back. Go to the Activity section of the Home page, and you'll see all the latest activity from the new Stumblers that you have a loose relationship with. Now comes the hard part. It's what separates the average Stumbler from the Superstar Stumbler.

Engaging other Stumblers

For one to three months, comment and like content that your fellow Stumblers are interacting with. In addition, share new content directly with your followers by clicking the Share icon — the square with an arrow going through it, as shown in Figure 10-7.

Now here's the kicker. Only share content with other Stumblers *from other sources* (not your original content) in the first one to three months. This tactic builds trust, as far too many people are only on StumbleUpon to promote their content from the beginning. Yes, promoting your content may be the eventual goal, but you have to create relationships first by helping others.

The next tactic you can use is to message those Stumblers who are following you and you are following them.

Figure 10-7: Share content with Stumblers that are following you by clicking the Share icon.

To see how this messaging would work, go to your Home page and then click the Profile link in the upper middle of the page. On your Profile page, click Followers below the StumbleUpon DNA section. You'll see a list of the Stumblers that follow you. Click a Stumbler to whom you'd like to send a message. Doing so brings up the Profile page of that Stumbler. Look for the small envelope icon to the left of his or her profile picture. Click the icon, and a New Message box appears, as shown in Figure 10-8. Type a message in the Message field and click Send, and your outreach attempt of the day is sent on its merry way.

Figure 10-8: To send a message to a Stumbler, click the envelope icon to bring up the New Message box.

Asking others to Stumble your content

If you've taken the previous steps for one to three months and beyond, you should have no problem with asking others to Stumble your content. You may do this using several communication methods:

- ✔ E-mail
- ✔ Other social networks
- ✔ Messaging other Stumblers

When using e-mail, come up with a general template to send to your list. It outlines what the benefits are to the people who will be consuming your content. Remember to put the focus on how it will benefit them, whether it's a new concept worth learning about or the fact that their audience will love the theme of the content.

As you can probably guess, StumbleUpon isn't the only social network out there, and you should have no problem asking your followers on other networks to Stumble your content. (This, of course, is based on the premise that you've developed solid relationships on those social networks in addition to StumbleUpon.)

Messaging Stumblers where there is a reciprocal following relationship, meaning that you both follow each other, is the best way to directly ask others to Stumble your content.

Finally, don't forget about Paid Discovery. You will see in the case study in this chapter's sidebar that shows how Paid Discovery has added benefits for forging new connections and getting your content in front of more people.

Now that you have a good sense of how to create content that Stumblers love and create meaningful relationships through sharing, it's time to put your newfound knowledge to work!

Celebrating success — A case study

To see the true value of using StumbleUpon to drive results for your website, check out how an indie music start-up called hypetree leveraged its StumbleUpon connections.

As an independent musician, hypetree cofounder Alex Mitchell grew frustrated with the lack of resources for indie artists to get discovered, so he created a venture to connect artists with people who love label-free music. The website compares the music of two independent bands and allows the fans to choose which songs they like better. hypetree has since expanded the service to include more bells and whistles.

As a start-up, hypetree really felt the pressure to validate market demand for such a service as hypetree, so it needed to drive traffic to its site so that people could sign up for the beta version.

hypetree wanted to get 1,000 users to sign up before its official product launch.

Results of Paid Discovery and Organic Traffic from StumbleUpon

Over 6,000 people signed up for the beta version within the first week of the campaign!

Campaign Details

- ✓ **Targeting:** Music, Indie Music, Internet, Internet Tools
- ✓ **Demographic:** M & F | 13 – 45 | USA
- ✓ **Total Visits:** 180,000+
- ✓ **Paid Visits:** 2,500
- ✓ **Earned Visits:** 179,000+
- ✓ **Total Sign-ups:** 6,000+
- ✓ **Campaign Score:** 90% (average is 75%)
- ✓ **Total Investment:** $125
- ✓ **Cost per Conversion:** 3¢

Chapter 11

Understanding StumbleUpon Etiquette

emember as a child when your parents taught you how to behave and act in a social setting?

Well, think of this chapter as your StumbleUpon parental guidance lesson as to how to conduct yourself when it comes to content in particular and using StumbleUpon in general. From the basics of appreciating the fact that you're not the only Stumbler in the StumbleUpon universe to realizing that too much of a good thing is not always good — after reading this chapter, you'll be another Emily Post or Miss Manners, at least in matters StumbleUpon-ish.

Realizing It's Not All about You

After you make your way onto StumbleUpon, you may feel the need or even the urge to promote and push only your content, all the time. Do yourself and all other Stumblers a favor and fight that urge and deny that need.

While you may have a great website where you write about all the latest goings-on in your particular world or industry, your fellow Stumblers do not want nor need to see every single one of your blog posts, articles, updates to your site, and so on (and on and on).

Instead of letting it all hang out, focus on only the "good stuff." And only you will know what that is. Push only the content that you're sure is going to whet your fellow Stumblers' appetite to learn more about you and your company, business, and so on.

So here's the moral: It's okay to push your content from time to time, but always remember the person on the other end of the line. He doesn't want to only see content specifically about you. He wants you to share with him some of the incredible content that you Stumble upon during the course of your day, just as you would want him to share with you.

Sharing the Right Content

So you know not to just share and push only your content, right? The next question then is "What is the right content to share on StumbleUpon?" Good question; glad you asked.

Unfortunately, no set answer exists. But here are some basic guidelines to adhere to when sharing content other than your own:

- ✔ **Follow the crowds:** Basically, look at what other people are sharing and follow their lead. After you log on to StumbleUpon.com, you can see the more popular Stumbles from those you are following to get a sense of what people are sharing.

    To do that, start out from your Home screen and click the Activity link near the upper right of the screen. Doing so brings up a page with the words `Activity from Stumblers and Lists You're Following` across the top. (See Figure 11-1.) Scan through the listings here to see what's hot — and what's not.

    When using the StumbleUpon app on your mobile device, you can see the most popular Stumbles by tapping the button labeled — you guessed it — Popular. Refer to Chapters 4 and 5 for using StumbleUpon on a mobile device.

- ✔ **Mix it up a little:** Don't just share the same kinds of content from the same sources over and over again — spice it up a little. Say, for example, you love content from the *Wall Street Journal* website. That's great. But chances are you can find articles about the same topics on other sites. Share them, too!

Figure 11-1: The Activities screen.

✔ **Know your fellow Stumblers:** After you are up and running on StumbleUpon and are following others and others are following you, you will get a sense of what to share.

You'll start to see patterns forming about what other Stumblers are sharing with you, and you can then use that information to hone in on what your fellow Stumblers want to see you share.

Overloading with too many shares

Nothing will get you taken off someone's list or unfollowed faster on StumbleUpon than sharing too many things in too short of a time frame. For example, if you're sharing say 10–12 different websites at the same time, that is way too many and is the classic definition of *information overload.*

Pace yourself, people. This is a marathon, not a sprint. Just like you wouldn't want so many shares sent your way at one time, neither does anyone else.

Another quick way to join the ranks of the unfollowed is to always share content from the same site. No matter how good you may think the content from that particular site may be, if people start to see the same site coming from you *all the time,* they may start to think that you're spamming them. And no one wants that.

Repeating the same share

Along the same lines of overloading with too many shares is the act of sending the same piece of content over and over and over and . . . you get the idea.

If you shared the same content repeatedly, say, for five or six times and no one Stumbled it after any of those offers, chances are that they're not going to Stumble it the next seven, eight, or nine more times you're thinking of sharing it again.

In some situations, repeating the same share is acceptable and may even be appreciated. For example, if you shared a piece of content on a potentially harmful virus a month prior and that same virus is still causing problems, resharing may help those who did not see your previous Stumble.

Creating Multiple Accounts

Spam truly is a four-letter word, and some unscrupulous Stumblers who, in an attempt to avoid being labeled as a spammer, will set up multiple StumbleUpon accounts.

Fortunately, you can spot these bad folks. For instance, anytime you receive the very same Stumble from four, five, or six different accounts, that's a pretty good sign that it is spam.

Another way to spot those spammers with multiple accounts is to take a close look at the names on the accounts when you do get those Stumbles mentioned previously. Oftentimes these spammers will use the same "root name" in all their accounts. For example, you could see VanillaBaby2, IceVanilla4U, and so on. (Hey, nobody said these folks were particularly bright.)

Note: These names were made up and any connection to any real StumbleUpon accounts is purely coincidental.

Cross-promoting on Other Networks

People will want to get maximum exposure for their content; that's not breaking news. As such, they'll often share content with you that may contain a link back to the original source — say, their website. However, they may also share content with a link that takes you to a social media site, such as Digg or Reddit, or even to a site that no one even knows exists.

All this "hidden agenda" self-/cross-promotion is yet another sure-fire way of getting unfollowed on StumbleUpon.

The best method for cross-promoting your content to multiple social networks is quite simply to give your readers the tools to navigate among your various platforms as easily as possible. Include Share buttons and options right on your site which include, of course, StumbleUpon and the aforementioned sites along with Facebook and Twitter.

Knowing When to Give a Thumbs Down

In Chapter 5, we invoke the name of the person most associated with the art of using a thumb to evoke emotion: Fonzie, or The Fonz if you prefer. Remember, if Fonzie liked something, it was thumbs up all the way. But, if he didn't, well it was thumbs down for whatever he disliked.

When using StumbleUpon, you have the chance to assert your inner Fonzie and give a website or Stumble a thumbs down. To do this, you first must have the StumbleUpon toolbar installed on your computer, or if you're using the StumbleUpon app on your mobile device, the Thumbs Down icon will be at the bottom of every page.

Check out Chapter 3 for more on how to install the StumbleUpon toolbar on your computer, and see Chapters 4 and 5 for using the StumbleUpon app on your mobile device.

After your toolbar is installed on your computer, you'll see a Thumbs Down icon at the top center of the screen. (See Figure 11-2.)

Figure 11-2: The Thumbs Down icon at top center of the StumbleUpon Home screen.

By giving content a thumbs down, you are in essence doing your part to help the folks at StumbleUpon.

You see, when you give a thumbs down, you're telling them what kind of content you don't want to see in the future. It also alerts StumbleUpon as to what content is spammy, has malware, or provides a less-than-satisfactory user experience.

Here are the choices you see when you click the Thumbs Down icon:

- ✔ **Not for Me:** While this particular content may not be right for you, it very well may be right for others.

- ✔ **Seen Page Already:** Just as you would expect, when you choose this option, it lets StumbleUpon know that you have in fact already seen this content.

- ✔ **Page Does Not Load:** For whatever reason, the website you are trying to view is not loading properly.

- ✔ **Report as Spam:** Selecting this one lets StumbleUpon know that not only do you not want to see this anymore, but it's also not suitable for any Stumbler, either.

- ✔ **Block:** Choosing this option will prevent any further content from this specific domain or website from ever appearing in your Stumbled content again.

Chapter 12

Ten Tips and Tricks from Power Users

*I*f you've made it this far, you should be fairly comfortable with all aspects of the StumbleUpon experience. Discovering and sharing content will never be the same again for you. Before we let you go, you need to hear from a few people.

We can't think of a better way to conclude this book than by show-casing advice that we've gathered from some of StumbleUpon's true power users!

Growing Your Network

To get the full benefit of the StumbleUpon community, you need to have an army of supporters. It's very similar to growing your network in real life. No one wants to talk to themselves, so they go and find people that are like-minded. The same is true for StumbleUpon. Your number-one goal in the beginning is to actively grow your network. How does one grow his/her network? Well, we're glad you asked.

Quite simply, you have to actively share content directly with other Stumblers. This is the number-one way to get on other users' radars. To find out more about how best to share content with other Stumblers, check out Chapter 7.

The StumbleUpon Toolbar Is There for a Reason — Use It!

The StumbleUpon toolbar is the most efficient way to use the social network, because it gives you instant access to StumbleUpon features on any page that you are on. So how do you make the best use of the toolbar?

To be quite honest, you have many uses for the toolbar, so we've put them into a list. Then you can try each task to see what works best for you. (Curious where all the icons are? See Figure 12-1.)

- ✔ **Stumble new pages by clicking the dark orange "Stumble" button.**

- ✔ **Like a page by clicking the Thumbs Up icon.** This means that you would like to see similar pages in the future. It will also store the page in the Likes section of your profile.

- ✔ **Add a page to one of your lists by selecting the plus sign.** Truly one of the best features of StumbleUpon, the ability to quickly add a page, helps you organize and save the pages you find particularly interesting all in one place. You can also add the same page to multiple lists.

- ✔ **Dislike a page using the Thumbs Down icon.** To spell out *why* you don't like the page, click the drop-down arrow and choose a reason from the menu that appears. Doing so helps improve your user-specific Stumble algorithm.

- ✔ **Share the page to Facebook by clicking the f-icon.** This option also lights up when you like a page.

- ✔ **Share the page on Twitter, on LinkedIn, through e-mail, or through StumbleUpon.** To share a page with another Stumbler, he or she must be following you.

- ✔ **See who has commented on or liked the page by clicking the Speech bubble.** Click the View All Comments link to open a new tab with all the user feedback the page has received, including Likes, Comments, and the lists it has been added to.

- ✔ **Click the drop-down menu at the upper-right corner to Stumble specific Interests, edit your current ones, or**

Stumble a different stream. This is also great when you want to check on the recent activity of the people you follow or on posts that are trending on StumbleUpon.

✔ **Check your shares, messages, or Stumble updates.** If you have anything new, it will show up as an orange number inside the green box near the right side. The number will stay orange until you open the page. If you don't have any new Shares or Messages, the number will be a white zero.

✔ **Return to the Home page by clicking the House icon.**

┌The StumbleUpon toolbar

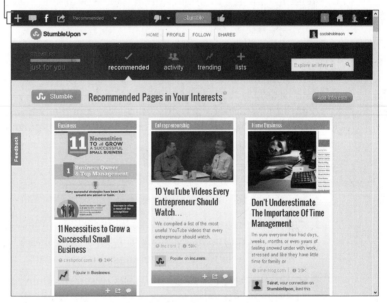

Figure 12-1: Be sure to "power use" the StumbleUpon toolbar.

Refer to Chapter 3 for more in-depth tips on using the StumbleUpon toolbar.

What Works — and What Doesn't — When Sharing

Anytime you find a piece of content that is truly remarkable, you're going to want to share it with your network. Here are some do's and don'ts when it comes to sharing content:

 ✔ Do share content that others will find valuable or entertaining.

 ✔ Don't share content that doesn't add value.

 ✔ Do share content with your StumbleUpon friends as well friends and followers on other social networks.

 ✔ Don't share content that could offend people.

 ✔ Do share content with e-mail contacts if they are not on StumbleUpon.

 ✔ Don't only share content that's designed to promote your site. Mix it up with third-party sources.

Refer to Chapter 7 for more great ideas about sharing content on StumbleUpon.

Using Paid Discovery

Paid Discovery can be a great tool for increasing the reach of your content when done correctly. Here are a couple of pointers to remember when setting up and running your campaigns:

 ✔ Define your goals at the start.

 ✔ Come up with a budget and stick to it.

 ✔ Be sure to target by interests.

 ✔ Tightly define the audience you're trying to reach.

 ✔ Tightly define what devices (desktop browsers, tablets, smart-phones) you want to target in each campaign.

 ✔ Check statistics on a daily basis to see whether you can make adjustments.

 ✔ Experiment with different content formats (that is, video, pictures, blog posts, web pages with audio, and so on).

Refer to Chapter 9 for more in-depth tips on setting up and improving Paid Discovery campaigns.

Sharing Great Content

Sharing great content is the most important tactic you have in your arsenal when it comes to increasing your reach on StumbleUpon. The trick is finding the right topics that the StumbleUpon community finds valuable.

Here is a step-by-step approach to sharing great content and evaluating your success:

1. **Share content that you find on the web.**

2. **Keep track of each share in an Excel spreadsheet.**

3. **Each month, go back and check to see what the Like and Share count is for each particular piece of content.**

    Also see if there are any comments directly related to your contribution.

4. **Identify content themes that perform well in the StumbleUpon community.**

5. **Rinse and repeat every month.**

Sharing Content with other Stumblers

To get your content seen and shared by other Stumblers (if you're not using Paid Discovery), you need to reach out to and share content with other Stumblers. Here is a step-by-step approach to sharing content with other Stumblers:

1. **Share and like Stumblers' content.**

2. **Connect with the Stumbler on other social networks like Twitter and Facebook.**

3. **Ask each Stumbler if the content is up their alley, and if they would like you to continue to share that type of content with them. (All through private messaging.).**

4. **Ask them to do the same if they're willing.**

Socializing on StumbleUpon

The best way to create social connections on StumbleUpon is to comment on what others have commented on. Comments often turn into full-blown conversations. This is a great way to get to know the community. Here are some best practices when socializing on StumbleUpon:

- ✔ Do leave comments on interesting pieces of content.
- ✔ Do interact with other commenters on a piece of content.

✔ Don't be rude or put anyone down for his/her comments.

✔ Don't be self-promotional with a link to your content. Keep the conversation focused on the subject — at the piece of content.

Finding Quality Content to Share

Finding quality content on StumbleUpon can be done in a number of ways. The easiest way is to click the orange Stumble button at the top of StumbleUpon.com.

You could also look in the trending section of StumbleUpon to see whether any pieces of content are worth sharing. Sometimes, you find a gem in the mix.

Finally, you should rely on the content Stumblers you're following are sharing. You started following them because they share great content, right?

Now it's your turn to take the tips you've learned in this book and put them to good use. Remember, it's what you put into StumbleUpon that will give you the results you're looking for!

Appendix

Brands, Sites, and Celebrities Who Use StumbleUpon Effectively

•••

ABC News

ABC News does a great job of diversifying the content on its StumbleUpon channel. It has everything from the expected (such as government and politics) to the somewhat different and surprising (including cricket and spirituality).

Figure A-1: ABC News keeps the news interesting.

Chelsea Handler

Keeping with the theme of her successful talk show, *Chelsea Lately,* the Chelsea Handler channel shares a lot of content on celebrities that is not necessarily politically correct — which is why her fans love the show and StumbleUpon channel.

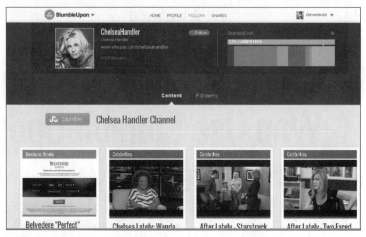

Figure A-2: Chelsea keeps things interesting, to say the least.

CNN

Much like ABC News, CNN has a wide array of content on its channel, ranging from general news to pop culture. CNN also has boards devoted to travel, crafts, and women's issues.

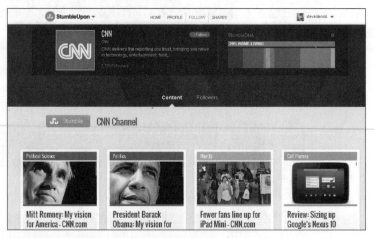

Figure AA-3: CNN News keeps the news interesting.

Cosmopolitan

Cosmo's channel description says it all: "Cosmopolitan is the channel for millions of fun, fearless females who want to be the best."

They even give the other half some time and share content dealing with men's issues.

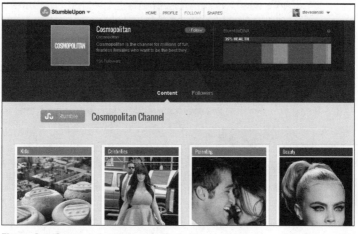

Figure A-4: Cosmo is keeping up with the times.

deviantART

deviantART was created to entertain, inspire, and empower the artist in all of us. Its StumbleUpon channel is truly a reflection of that, with content spanning every possible form of art you can imagine.

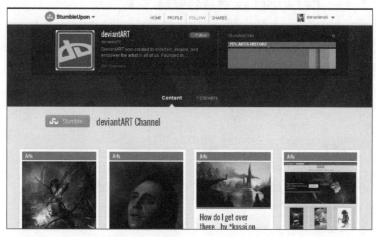

Figure A-5: deviantART is for the artist in you.

Funny or Die

Funny Or Die is a comedy video website that combines user-generated content with original, exclusive content — including content from celebrities. Its StumbleUpon channel is an extension of its website, featuring its wild and wacky take on no-holds-barred content.

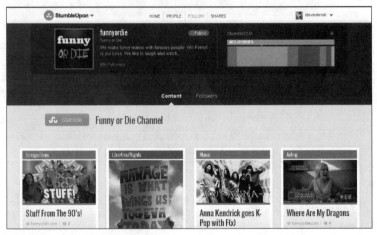

Figure A-6: Funny? You decide!

The History Channel

Anytime you use the word *history* without referencing a specific time in history, you know you're talking about a whole lot of content. The History Channel's channel is full of content relating to ages from many moons ago right up to the present day.

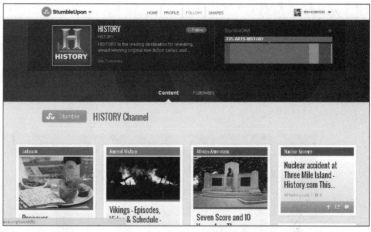

Figure A-7: Brush up on a little history on the History channel.

Jim Carrey

Being one of the funniest people on the planet means that people expect you to, well, be funny and to share funny content. The Jim Carrey channel is more than happy to oblige by sharing content on comedy movies (of course) plus other topics — all of them sharing the red thread of laughter running through them.

Figure A-8: Jim Carrey expands his comedic reach with the Jim Carrey channel.

Mashable

Being a leading source for news, information, and resources for the Connected Generation means sharing content that runs the gamut of all that surrounds us in the digital world we live in. And Mashable does not disappoint.

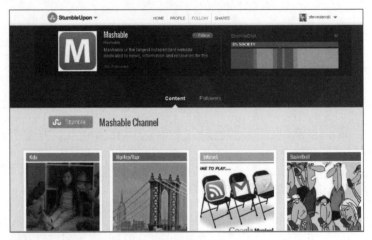

Figure A-9: How the Connected Generation gets its news.

StumbleUpon

You didn't think I'd pass on this one, did you? As diverse as the mother site is itself, the StumbleUpon channel serves up content guaranteed to satisfy any content appetite.

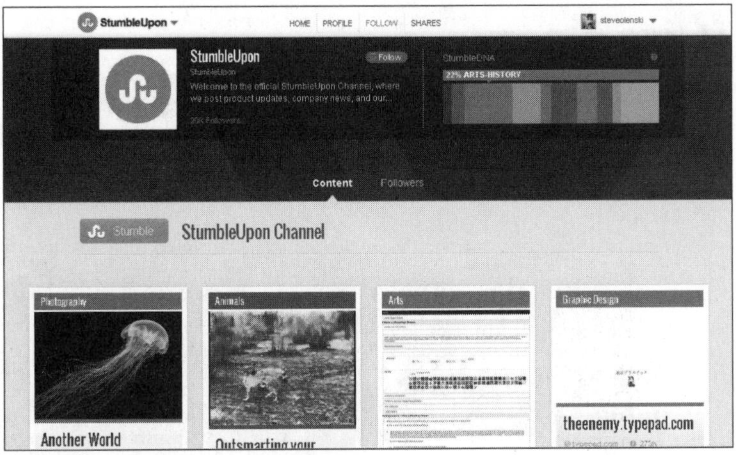

Figure A-10: StumbleUpon? But of course!

Time

Much like the magazine itself, the Time channel on StumbleUpon offers a taste of just about everything you can think of — and then some. Law, sports, global politics, punk rock, and even marine biology are just a few examples.

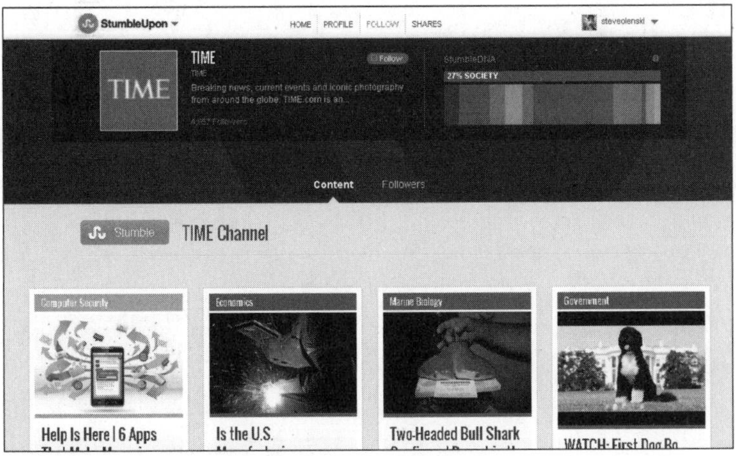

Figure A-11: Time has its own StumbleUpon channel.

Wired.com

A technology-focused website means a technology-focused StumbleUpon channel, right? Right. And Wired.com's channel delivers with plenty of techno-content but it also mixes in some not-so-techie content, as well.

Figure A-12: Stay wired with the Wired channel.

Index

About the Author

Steve Olenski is a severely over-caffeinated creative, imaginative, and passionate writing professional, specializing in all aspects of advertising, marketing, social media, content development, innovative thinking, and idea generation. He's been named one of the top 100 most influential people in social media by *Social Technology Review* and a top 50 blogger by Kred.

A member of the editorial board for the *Journal of Digital & Social Media Marketing,* Steve is currently a senior creative content strategist at Responsys, a leading global provider of on-demand e-mail and cross-channel marketing solutions.

Nick Robinson is a technology enthusiast, entrepreneur, and social media practitioner, having worked in the online marketing industry since the early days. He's owned several businesses, from website development to event services to consulting. He enjoys running and lacrosse when he's not burning the midnight oil.

By day, Nick Robinson is a social media channel manager at SAP, a world leader in enterprise software and software-related services.

Dedication

Steve would like to dedicate this book to his two children, Samantha and Josh, and his rock, a.k.a. his wife, Terri. If it weren't for Terri, Steve would still be living in his parents' basement. Not that there's anything wrong with that.

Nick would like to dedicate this book to his mother and father and two brothers, James and Chip. Without all the support and love for all these years, he wouldn't be where he is today.

Authors' Acknowledgments

The authors would like to acknowledge everyone who was so instrumental in helping them write this book. We would in particular like to thank the *For Dummies* team, including Amy Fandrei and Paul Levesque, for their guidance and patience. This was most assuredly a collaborative effort from start to finish.

Publisher's Acknowledgments

Acquisitions Editor: Amy Fandrei

Senior Project Editor: Paul Levesque

Copy Editor: John Edwards

Technical Editor: Keith Underdahl

Editorial Assistant: Annie Sullivan

Sr. Editorial Assistant: Cherie Case

Project Coordinator: Patrick Redmond

Cover Image: Home office: © horiyan / iStockphoto; Runner: © Adam Turner / iStockphoto; Vegetables: © Liv Friis-Larsen / iStockphoto; Family: © Christopher Futcher / iStockphoto; Landscape: © Brian Raisbeck / iStockphoto